WRITING IN PSYCHOLOGY

WRITING IN PSYCHOLOGY

A GUIDEBOOK

by

Charles Allen Gramlich
Y. Du Bois Irvin
Elliott D. Hammer

THE BORGO PRESS

An Imprint of Wildside Press LLC

MMIX

Borgo Literary Guides
ISSN 0891-9623

Number Twelve

www.wildsidepress.com

FIRST EDITION

CONTENTS

DEDICATIONS

To Jeff Stripling, teacher, advisor and friend—Charles Gramlich

To W. E. Burghardt Du Bois, mentor, beloved grandfather, and the first person to stimulate my interests in languages, reading, and writing—Y. Du Bois Irvin

To Paul Dykes, Mike Kimrey, and Janet B. Ruscher, who taught me to think and write, occasionally both at the same time—Elliott D. Hammer

ACKNOWLEDGMENTS

We would like to thank all the students at Xavier University of Louisiana who have taken the course for which this book was originally written, and who have provided us with feedback over the years. That help has been greatly appreciated.

INTRODUCTION

"When the only tool you own is a hammer,
every problem begins to resemble a nail."
—Abraham Maslow

A good way to introduce this book might be to ask you, the reader, a question. Why do you want—or need—to learn how to write? Is it to communicate important information, or to amaze and amuse your friends, or because you want to get good grades in the classroom? Maybe you just want to get rich? These are all legitimate reasons for writing. In fact, there are *no* illegitimate reasons to write. Each writer has his or her own purpose and own unique way of working toward that purpose. Ernest Hemingway often wrote standing up (Lynn, 1987). Truman Capote and Mark Twain preferred lying down to write, while Edgar Allan Poe liked to wear his cat on his shoulder while he scribed his poetry (Fryxell, 2001). You'll create your own path, of course.

Given the many reasons for writing, and the many ways of going about the process, how does one decide what to put into a guidebook like this one? Well, we started by eliminating all but one reason for writing, and that is writing to communicate information. This does not mean that other reasons are less important or less "good." It just means that we had to focus somewhere, and the transmission of ideas is basic to *all* writing. (No one gets rich from writing unless he or she can convey something interesting to a large number of people.) We also know that grades are important, but learning how to use writing for effective communication will lead directly to better grades.

Many college students do not particularly enjoy writing and might find the idea of reading a book on the topic unpleasant, but writing is a skill that everyone needs. Most people *can* write, but not many do it really well and those who do are in demand. And the kind of scientific writing that professional psychologists do, and which is expected of students in both undergraduate and graduate psychology programs, has its own requirements and its own set of specialized skills.

Even if you are already a good writer, this book will help you become better. It should especially help you become adept at communicating thoughts on paper in the way that a psychologist would. That process involves thinking about writing, and practice at writing. It begins on the next page. Enjoy!

CHAPTER ONE

CONCEPTS

"I'm sorry to have written such a long letter.
I did not have time to write a short one."
—George Bernard Shaw

We said in the introduction that writing well requires thinking about writing and practice at writing. This chapter focuses on the "thinking" part of that process. To begin with, we need to understand the strengths and weaknesses of writing, and the strengths and weaknesses that writers of all kinds bring to their work. The concepts we would like to cover in this chapter are, 1) writing as it differs from talking, 2) taking the time to write well, 3) developing the attitudes and habits of good writers, 4) developing confidence in your writing, and 5) avoiding the trap of perfection. These are all concepts that will appear again and again in this book. They're discussed separately in the sections that follow.

Writing and Talking

Writing and talking are two ways of communicating ideas. Talking is more familiar to most of us, and it's very common for people to write much like they talk. Although this is fine for a personal letter to a friend, or even for the first draft of a more formal paper, it is not good enough for a letter to a prospective employer, or for a paper that has to be handed in for a grade. Formal writing—what this book is about—is not the same as talking, and this causes us some enormous difficulties but also brings us some enormous benefits.

To get a feel for the way people talk, try listening to a casual conversation among your friends. Don't eavesdrop. Just listen for a while instead of talking. Notice the insertions of "uh" or "you know" into the conversation, the short pauses while someone tries to think of something to say, the interruptions as one person cuts off another.

Spoken language gets its message across, but there are always false starts, considerable backtracking, and the use of "reactive" speech, which means that each person's response builds upon information just provided by the other person. Written language cannot proceed this way, both because it looks confusing on the printed page ("I...uh... you know...we wanted"), and because there is only one person present at a time, first the writer and then the reader.

Another thing that is true of talking—but not of writing—is that there is a substantial amount of non-verbal communication involved in a spoken exchange. Emphasizing words can be done with hand gestures, punching the air with a fist or pointing a finger, and indecisiveness can be shown with a shrug. People can judge how clearly their points are being made by watching other people's facial expressions, rushing on at smiles and nods, backtracking at frowns and head shakes. A spoken conversation uses body movements for punctuation and is filled with immediate feedback on the speaker's success, or lack of it, in conveying a message. This just doesn't happen in writing—though question marks and other punctuation symbols are a feeble attempt to add some of the same information.

The audience that you are writing for might be in the next city, or the next state, or the next country. They can't shake their heads at you if they fail to understand something you tell them. This is the major weakness of writing, and because of it you have to think about what you are saying much more carefully when writing than when talking.

If you say something confusing while chatting with someone, then it takes very little energy for them to ask a question. But if you confuse someone who is reading your words, the easiest thing for them to do is either tune out the message and just scan the piece, or to throw it aside and turn to something else. These are not good outcomes, particularly if the individual reading your work is the same person who is going to grade it. To communicate effectively on paper you have to anticipate questions the reader might ask, and then provide him or her with everything needed to answer those questions.

What kind of questions do readers ask? Here are two good ways to find out. First, develop your own reading habit, and especially cultivate the ability to read critically. For example, you've probably found confusing paragraphs in textbooks before. Chances are you asked someone to explain the passages, or just skipped over them to something easier. Critical reading means not skipping the confusing stuff. It means asking *why* those passages are confusing. Is it you? Or did the writer do something wrong? Often, you'll find that the writer left out some important piece of information that the reader needed to know. By reading critically and examining other people's mistakes, you can begin to see the kind of things that a writer needs to do to communicate effectively.

A second way to find out what readers need from writers is to let some friends read your paper and indicate where it confused them. Choose those friends carefully, though. Don't pick people who will only brag on your writing. Good as that might be for your ego, it won't help you earn a better grade on a paper. Pick people who will be honest, and then listen to them with an open mind and without getting defensive about the work. When a friend mentions something that confused them, don't try to "talk" them through an explanation. The writing has to explain itself, and if it doesn't then the writer hasn't quite done his or her job.

Taking criticism is not easy, but it is absolutely necessary if you are going to get better. This doesn't mean you have to agree with everything that readers say in a critique, but it does mean that you should give their comments careful consideration. Be sure to pay special attention to items that *several* people point out as a problem. Where there's a consensus among the readers there's likely to be an error by the writer.

Taking Time to Write Well

Lack of immediate feedback is the worst thing about writing. But, on the positive side, there are no "uh's" cluttering up written work. There is no other person to jump in and interrupt your argument before you even decide what that argument is. The best thing about writing, and the most powerful tool of the medium, is that there is *time*, time to think and time to tinker.

The words exist on a sheet of paper or a computer screen in front of you, and no one else in the world knows they are there. Think about the enormous freedom this provides. You can say anything without fear of contradiction or of being laughed at. You can try all kinds of ways of putting down information, and then, if you need or want to, you can throw it all away and never let anyone see it. Is this not a liberating concept? It means there is *never* any reason not to start writing. No possible harm can come from it.

Of course, much of the material written for classes has to be handed in to teachers. But, if you don't wait until the last minute to start writing a paper there will still be enough time to change things around until they're just the way you want them. This process of thinking about ideas, then changing them, and maybe even discarding them, is pretty much the same as what we do in spoken conversations. The main difference is that with writing no one is waiting impatiently for us to say something, and, in fact, we have the luxury of thinking out an entire argument before exposing it to anyone.

Although "time" is the biggest advantage of writing over speaking, it is not a tool that is used as much as it should be. Many of the papers that teachers get in their classes are really first efforts, and they read almost like spoken conversations. They lack complete sentences, or else have long sentences that try to do too much work. They have important information that is out of place, put at the end, for example, when it should have been at the beginning.

What happens is that student writers often put down their thoughts immediately as those thoughts occur, and then do not bother to go back and rearrange them into a consistent and logical whole. This takes away the advantage of writing but leaves the handicap of not having feedback from a conversational partner. Good writing is really rewriting. You have to work with the first draft, changing things around, adding and deleting things, polishing. Ever say something and then want to take it back because it wasn't exactly what you meant? In writing, up until that final draft is handed in, you *can* take it back.

Writing Attitudes & Habits

There are as many ways to write as there are writers. Some writers work in the morning, others in the evening. Some writers write to music; some need quiet. Most writers write as part of another job, whether they are lawyers writing reports, teachers writing articles, or students writing term papers. The important point is that they all *do* write. There is no substitute for sitting down and pounding out the words.

Writing takes both skill and discipline, and, of the two, discipline is more important. In fact, almost everyone probably has the basic verbal skills needed to write; most humans grow up with language and use it every day. Why, then, do some people find it easier to write than others? A big part of the answer has to do with discipline. Disciplining oneself to write requires a few basic attitudes and habits. These are discussed in the following paragraphs.

Attitude 1: Make writing important to you. To do a good job of writing, it has to be a task that you value, a task for which you are willing to sacrifice—at least a little. There are many things that you probably like to do, and using time for writing means having less time to do those things, whether they be watching TV, reading novels, or chatting with friends. If you don't believe that writing is important, then you'll only turn attention to it at odd hours, when friends are asleep and there is nothing good on TV. These are also the hours when you are likely to be tired, or bored, neither of which makes for good writing.

So how do you make writing important to yourself? Well, do so by realizing the benefits it can bring. Some people just like the process of writing, the simple act of putting words down on a page and then changing them around. And that is the best attitude to have. But, if you cannot enjoy the process, then learn to value the finished product. Being able to write well translates into good grades in college, and, once out on the job market, into money. Good writers get more ready acceptance into graduate and professional schools, better entry level positions when they start their careers, and more rapid promotions. Good writing pays dividends.

Attitude 2: Write about something interesting. Ever hear another student say: "I have to do a term paper in my history/psychology/business class but I just can't find anything interesting to write about." Teachers hear this all the time too, and we hate it because college is a time to be interested in everything. In college, students are *required* to explore a variety of topics, and for many people it will be the last time they'll have that experience.

Let's say, though, that you really detest history but have to do a term paper for a history class. What do you do? The answer is, find something about history that you like. Every activity that you *do* enjoy has a history, whether it be playing chess, cooking gourmet meals, or writing poetry. Even TV has a history. Be creative in picking a topic and you need not be bored.

But what if the teacher assigns topics and you end up with "The Story of the Senate" or "The History of the American Political System?" The same advice holds. There are many ways of approaching any subject, including American politicians and American politics. If you find people's personal lives interesting, then remember that politicians eat, drink, and fool around just like everyone else. They fight among themselves. They commit crimes and get involved in scandals. Maybe these elements can help identify a focus for your paper. Certainly try to work this kind of information in among the dryer facts that you *have* to cover. Never let the paper win before you start to fight. Make the topic work for instead of against you.

Habit 1: Make time for writing. No one can write unless they have time to sit and think. But if you wait for time to find you, it never will. You make time for going to the movies, time for watching TV. You also have to make time for writing, and the easiest way to do that is to first draw up a schedule of your activities and find out where the free time is. Using Appendix A's sample schedule, take an honest look at your daily routine. Then, depending on the length of your writing project, mark out a few hours a week—or more—for writing. Maybe there's a free hour between your afternoon classes, or use an hour before bed on Tuesdays and Thursdays. Once writing time is scheduled, use that time consistently for work on a writing project. Do not download music during that time. Do not surf the internet. Write.

Some people have suspected Stephen King of hiring a ghost writer because he is so prolific. However, he claims that his typical modest output—about 2,000 words a day, or seven to eight pages—is plenty to turn out a 180,000 word novel in three months (King, 2000). He is, of course, consistent and rarely misses a day. And he doesn't quit typing until he meets his self-imposed quota of words.

In a student's hectic schedule, it's sometimes difficult to squeeze in regular time for writing, but time and regularity is essential to doing a decent job. Stephen King can't write a good novel in a week. Most students can't write a good term paper in a day. Waiting until a deadline is looming before starting means that you'll be planning in advance *not* to do your best work. We don't mean necessarily that the paper will get an "F," but we can guarantee that you won't have done your best work, and you may never learn how talented a writer you really are.

Like King, don't try to finish your writing project all at once. Set aside a manageable amount of time each week for working on the computer, and then stick to it. It's all right to occasionally work a little under or a little past your scheduled time, but don't cut yourself too much slack and don't write to exhaustion. Consistency *over* time is the key. (See Chapter 6 for more discussion on time management.)

Habit 2: Look up things about which you are unsure. Learn to keep a dictionary and a grammar guide close at hand while writing (see Bibliography). Not sure of a word's meaning? Look it up. Can't recall how a semicolon is used? Look it up. Almost everything a writer needs to know is already written down somewhere. Some of it is in this book. Make a habit of checking yourself against such sources. This will take effort at first—the easiest thing is to be lazy—but it'll soon become routine. And it'll become less and less necessary as your abilities improve.

Habit 3: Do multiple drafts of everything. The habit that might improve your writing the most is to *rewrite* everything. Just assume that any first draft is a mess and that it is not good enough to hand in. Do it over again. This seems like work, and that's exactly what it is. But, after all, you would never expect to build a perfect chair the first time you tried carpentry, would you? Even if you did, you would still have to sand it, and polish it, and paint it. Writing is the same way. No one builds a perfect paper the first time through. (See Chapter 9 for much more on rewriting.)

Habit 4: Use writing as a way of challenging yourself. Any job that is done over and over in exactly the same way is going to get boring after a while. Never let this happen to your writing. Within a paper, vary the lengths of sentences and paragraphs. Find synonyms for words that are used several times. Play games, like trying to cut a word from each paragraph of the final draft. Between papers, try out new ways of organizing material. Vary the words, the tone, the punctuation. Take risks. All these things will help you improve as a writer, and that's the goal.

Habit 5: Read. This is something that was mentioned earlier in this book but it certainly deserves another hearing. Quite simply, good writers are also good readers. This doesn't mean they read only classics. More likely, it means that they read a little bit of everything, novels, textbooks, journals, magazines, newspapers, the backs of cereal boxes. Reading furnishes the ideas and facts needed for term papers, but it also gives the reader a sense of language, of how words are used. The more you read, the better you'll write.

Developing Confidence

We've discussed writing and talking, taking the time to write well, and the attitudes and habits of good writers. Now we turn to the subject of "confidence." By this, we mean feeling secure in your knowledge of a subject and your ability to deal with it in writing. This is often lacking in those who are relatively new to writing, and it can lead to avoidance of the whole process, or, occasionally, to serious problems like plagiarism (stealing someone else's words and ideas).

Confidence is crucial to writing, and there is absolutely no way to gain confidence without trying and succeeding. You may have to modify your idea of success, though, at least at first. Don't expect to sit down and write a perfect essay on the first attempt. It won't work out that way. With practice, you may start getting closer to a good draft on the first try, but it will take a while to get to that point, as it has for everyone who writes.

Certainly do not expect your first polished efforts to be publishable. Even if a paper earns an "A" in class it is highly unlikely that anyone is going to pay for the privilege of publishing it. Instead, start out with modest goals that can be easily met, like finishing that first paper, or learning a new word and using it correctly, or improving your grammar and punctuation. Once you've gained confidence from meeting these simple goals, then select tougher goals for the next paper. Do not try to improve everything at once.

In addition, remember that we often get a mistaken impression about how talented other people are. We pick up a novel and think how superbly written it is. We hear a good lecture from a teacher and we think, "Wow, this lady really knows her stuff." We see LeBron James slam-dunk a basketball and we just stare. In each case we think how lucky some people are to be born with those kinds of skills. And in each case we are wrong.

Sure, LeBron would probably be better at basketball than most of us even if he had never practiced it. But all of us could be better than we are if we worked hard enough at it. People are not born experts. They may have innate talents, like size, speed, or coordination, but most people have to work hard to make their jobs look easy. Writing is the same. Being a good writer is probably both a gift and a learned skill. Some people *may* just be better than others. But almost everyone can learn to write a term paper that will earn an "A" in college, and *anyone* can dramatically improve their writing with some thought and practice.

One of the keys to gaining confidence is knowing, beyond a shadow of a doubt, that you understand what you are writing about. As an exercise for this chapter, compose a short essay about something you know how to do very well. It might be how to change a flat tire, or how to barbecue, or how to work an iPod. This kind of exercise can occasionally be difficult because one has to put into words things that are normally done automatically. However, it should also illustrate one effect of knowing a subject. You don't have to worry about getting the facts correct or about someone pointing out a mistake.

Finally, remember that not even professors know everything about their subjects. Although some teachers might not want students to realize this, it should be relatively easy to find something your teacher doesn't know.

Psychology has grown so explosively that already by 1987 an average of 100 papers were published each *day* in the field (Schultz & Schultz). At that rate, not even a professional is going to keep up with every new development. Surely you could find the *one* or *two* articles your teacher missed. This should not give you a feeling of superiority, but it should give one of confidence.

Realize that professors and students are both involved in the process of learning. Professors might be a little further along the route than their students are, but they've been working at it longer. You can master the material, and then can write about it as easily as you can write about how to fix toast. It may require a considerable amount of reading, and several days of hard work, but it is not beyond your talents.

Breaking Down the Barriers and Reducing Anxiety

Sometimes it is difficult just to get started writing, whether it be the first words of a new paper or just the first words of the day on an older one, but there are techniques that can help. Most professionals develop ways to help them start a day's writing and keep up momentum on any piece they're working on. Some of these, from your authors and from Dana Dunn (Dunn, 2001), a psychologist and excellent writer, are given in the following paragraphs.

1. Write Badly at First. Occasionally, the block that keeps us from being productive is the fear of writing something that isn't good, or of wasting our time having to rewrite. As we have stressed before in this book, and will stress again later, rewriting is essential to a good paper, so forget about writing a perfect draft on the first pass. When working on that first draft, allow it to be terrible. Use incomplete sentences, leave gaps where you don't yet know enough, leave citations incomplete. Do whatever you have to do to get the important ideas down. The problems can always be fixed when you come back to the paper, and you will have recorded your ideas before they vanish.

2. Turn Off Your Monitor. One way to remove the anxiety of writing is to prevent yourself from *seeing* what you are writing. A simple way to do this is just turn the monitor off while writing. Or, if you work on a laptop try covering the monitor with a sheet of paper so that you can't read what is on the screen, or try writing with a white font on a white background. When you turn the monitor back on, or remove the cover, or turn the font to black, you'll be able to see what needs changing but will have reduced your inhibitions about making errors during the *act* of writing.

3. Leave Yourself Notes. Before ending a day's writing, jot down a few rough notes in the file itself about what you're thinking and where you plan to go next. This way, you won't have that awful feeling of sitting down for your next writing session and wondering, "Now, where was I?" Your past self is there to remind you.

In fact, while working through a paper leave yourself notes all along the way. Point out where more information is needed, where the writing is weak, where examples might best be used. Anything that helps you think about the topic and how to present it is worthwhile. By the way, it's best to leave those hints in a different colored font so that they're easy to locate. Your authors tend to make our own notes in red, but use whatever color gets your attention.

Avoiding the Trap of Perfection

There is one last concept in this chapter that you need to learn. Sometimes, try as we might, we are just unable to raise our writing to the level where we'd like it to be. Few of us are capable of stellar writing all the time, so let yourself off the hook. Avoid the trap of trying to make your writing perfect. This doesn't mean to let laziness keep you from correcting errors that you know exist, but it does mean that there comes a time when the paper is as good as it is going to get with your current level of skill.

There may still be some errors, problems with transitions or wordings, mistakes in grammar or punctuation. But remember that teachers expect undergraduate students to make mistakes. What they also expect is that students learn from their mistakes and do not just repeat the same error over and over. Do the best job you can, then hand the paper in and turn your mind elsewhere.

Conclusions

What are the concepts again that we've discussed in this chapter? First, writing is not the same as talking. You cannot depend on the cues of facial expression and body language for help. This means that one has to think more carefully and completely when writing than when talking.

Second, the big advantage of writing is that you have time to work out what you want to say before anyone sees it. If you say something wrong in a conversation, then it's said and cannot be taken back. But if you make a mistake in the early drafts of a paper, just erase it.

Third, you have to have discipline to write well. Make writing an important part of your college career. Learn to look things up in the dictionary or other reference works. Learn to rewrite. Read.

Fourth, set reasonable goals so that reaching those goals will help you gain confidence in your writing ability. The best way to build confidence is to know as much as possible about your subject.

Fifth, do the best job you can and never let laziness force you into handing in work that is mediocre, but also remember that you are going to make mistakes. Just learn from those mistakes and go on.

In closing, one more point that we would like to make is that a writing job is not really finished when the last draft is handed in to the teacher. In most cases, the teacher will return the paper with comments and a grade. The grade is the less important of the two; it can't be changed now. The comments, however, can help you get a better grade on that next paper, but only if you go over them carefully to see where your mistakes were made.

Most teachers end their year with at least a few student papers that no one even bothered to come by and pick up. Clearly, these students did not care very much about their work. And they are likely to go on making the same mistakes in every future paper they write.

Imagine for a moment being put into a strange room with a blindfold on, and then being given a basketball and told to shoot it into a hoop. The only problem is that no one explains where the goal is. One could shoot for days without getting any closer to scoring. Just a few hints, however, would be immensely helpful. If someone would just say "warmer" or "colder" after each shot, imagine the improvement it would make in your performance. The point is: how can you expect to do better on your next paper if you don't know what was right or wrong with the last paper? Teachers want to provide that feedback. Care enough to pay attention to it.

CHAPTER TWO

A BRIEF LOOK AT APA STYLE

True ease in writing comes from art, not chance,
As those move easiest who have learn'd to dance.
'Tis not enough no harshness gives offence,—
The sound must seem an echo to the sense.
                              —Alexander Pope

"APA Style" is a system devised by the American Psychological Association (APA) to help authors prepare clear and unbiased manuscripts for submission to journals. Its major intent is to aid researchers who are seeking publication for their work, but it can also serve as a model for students who want their college papers to communicate effectively, and to earn good grades. Even experienced writers rarely know all the "rules" of APA style. They keep the APA's written manual handy for reference, and so should you. That manual should be dog-eared by the time you graduate because you should constantly question what you "know" about writing and refer frequently to the manual for advice.

In 2001, the APA revised their style guide, which is currently known as the *Publication Manual of the American Psychological Association* (5th Edition). The information contained within the *Manual* was "drawn from an extensive body of psychological literature, from editors and authors experienced in psychological writing, and from recognized authorities on publication practices" (APA, 2001, p. XXIII). The resulting "style" is broadly accepted by a majority of readers and writers within the field of psychology.

[NOTE: The APA has plans to publish a 6th edition of the *Publication Manual*. This will expand the example sections of the *Manual* and provide more guidelines for working with online resources. Your *Guidebook* refers only to the currently available 5th edition of the *Manual* (APA, 2001). Although page numbers may change in the 6th edition, the basic information discussed here is likely to remain much the same.]

The *Publication Manual* (APA, 2001) provides serious students in psychology (and, indeed, in many disciplines within the Social Sciences) with a marvelous tool for improving their writing. Among this tool's benefits are:

1. It provides guidelines on how to get the most from the book by including a section on "how to use the *Publication Manual*." This is in the Introduction, which many people skip because they think it's superfluous. It isn't. Definitely read it.

2. It offers tips on organizing a paper and provides examples and illustrations that let writers get a visual "feel" for how their paper should look.

3. It is an excellent guide for helping writers avoid inaccuracies, unclear expressions, and ungrammatical sentences. It includes information on correct punctuation, spelling, and capitalization, as well as notes on abbreviations, headings, and the use of quotations.

4. Because the APA is committed to both science and sensitivity, the *Publication Manual* has significant sections on the issue of bias in language. The absence of grammatical error is *not enough*! It is important to habitually avoid language that is racist, sexist or that promotes ethnic bias.

For example, despite what some people think, using the generic "he" in writing is inappropriate except when referring to a male; the APA considers the term sex-specific. Also, both "Black" and "African American" *are* appropriate, as are "White" and "European American," but note that *Black* and *White* should be capitalized, and that *African American* and *European American* should not be hyphenated. Such is the level of detail required for sound writing in APA style.

5. Finally, the *Publication Manual* helps writers produce their papers in a uniform style that makes the editor's job easier, whether that editor is someone who works at a scientific journal or is the teacher in a class. Making an editor's job easier will increase the chances for publication at a journal, or of earning a good grade on a term paper in a course.

A short list of general instructions for APA style include:

• Double-space between *all* lines within a paper. (Note: many of the examples in this *Guidebook* will be single-spaced, which is common in published works to save space. Double-space *your* manuscripts, though.)

• Use one inch margins on *every* side. Make the left margin flush and allow the right margin to remain uneven.

• Don't break words into syllables at the end of a sentence.

• Number *all* pages consecutively in the upper right-hand corner, after the manuscript page header.

• Don't (or *do not*) use contractions, such as *don't, let's, can't.* (See "Authors' Comment" on the next page.)

• Pay attention to "person." Don't write in second person (avoid the use of "you"), and avoid the use of "I" or "we" except in rare cases. (See Authors' Comment again.)

• Pay attention to tense. When discussing a past finding, use past tense [*e.g.*, "Johnson (1998) found that participants quickly learned to avoid electrical shocks"], but when discussing a current phenomenon, use present tense [*e.g.*, "Johnson (1998) notes that shock avoidance appears to be innate"]. Finally, use future tense almost exclusively for hypotheses [*e.g.*, "The present study hypothesizes that low self-esteem participants will report greater aversion to the electrical shocks than will high self-esteem participants"] or in the Discussion section of a paper, where future research is discussed.

Authors' Comment: *You might be asking yourself why we're using contractions and the second person, "you," in this* Guidebook *if it violates APA style. Well, while we are conforming to the APA's* Publication Manual *(APA, 2001) for almost everything else, we wanted this book to feel more like a conversation between our readers and us, so we've allowed ourselves to be a little less formal. Term papers and journal articles need to be less familiar and more formal.*

Types of Articles and Their Parts

Three basic types of articles can appear in scientific journals—review articles, theoretical articles, and research reports. Review articles summarize, compare, contrast, and evaluate previously published material on a particular topic. They often include a final section where the writer suggests avenues for future research. Most term papers fit into this review article category, and though many "research reports" include a short review article within them, most journals do not publish review articles by themselves.

Theoretical articles resemble review articles but focus more on the advancement or critique of a particular theory.

These are usually written by established experts within a field. They do much more than just summarize and evaluate previous research, and are the most difficult of the three types to write. They require the most generalized knowledge.

Research reports make up the vast majority of material published by most scientific journals. Such reports consist of detailed notes on "why" and "how" an empirical (research) study was carried out, and they describe the results of the study with a discussion about how those results relate to current thinking within the field. Furthermore, the results are usually reported in statistical form and are often accompanied by figures and graphs.

Research reports have the most rigid format restrictions of the three types, and almost all contain the following parts: Title Page, Abstract, Introduction, Method, Results, Discussion, References, Tables, Figures. Review articles do not need the Method and Results sections, and they combine the Introduction and Discussion. They often lack Tables and Figures as well, although there is no reason why they can't contain them.

For students, a research report often begins life as a research *proposal*. Professors assign these to undergraduate students in methods classes to help them gain experience at planning a study or experiment. They are similar to research reports, except that they *propose* an original research study that has not been done instead of reporting on one that has. They may require an "Analysis" section, in which the statistics that will be used to analyze a study's results are described, as opposed to a Results section where those results are actually reported.

In the sub-titled sections that follow, the purpose for each part of the "research report" is discussed. For those who are reading this book mainly for help with term papers, we've indicated which sections can be left out or modified for a typical review article/term paper.

Title Page

The Title Page is the first thing editors (or instructors) see when they get a paper. It is an important part of an article and will need to appear in any term paper. The *Publication Manual* of the APA specifies how to format the Title Page (check the *Manual*'s subject index for "Title Page"), and there is a sample paper within the *Manual* that shows what it should look like. (Note: the sample paper provides a handy quick reference for many elements of APA style.)

For those of you writing term papers, please pay attention to what is *not* on the Title Page. Unless instructed otherwise, do not include a teacher's name. Do not write the date that the assignment was completed. Just space down ten to fifteen lines from the top and center the complete title, your name, and the complete name of your school. The following is an example.

Multiple Groups Needs Assessment Procedures in
Community Mental Health Settings
James K. Student
Xavier University of Louisiana

Several lines above the title and flush left there appears a "running head," which is an abbreviated or shortened title written in all capital letters that is chosen to reflect the full title. The running head cannot exceed 50 characters, with spaces and punctuation, and one possible running head from the example given in the previous paragraph would be "ASSESSMENT PROCEDURES." This would appear after the typed phrase "Running head:" (See the index in the *APA Manual* for page numbers where the "running head" is discussed).

Also appearing on *every* manuscript page, including the Title Page, is the "manuscript page header." This phrase contains the first two or three words of the title—even if those words don't make sense on their own—followed by five spaces and the page number. This "header" allows editors to reassemble a manuscript if the pages get separated during review. For the example we've been using, "Multiple Groups" or "Multiple Groups Needs" would be the only acceptable headers.

Abstract

Although the Title Page is the first thing a reader sees, the first thing he or she actually reads may well be the Abstract, which is a concise but comprehensive summary of a paper's contents. Research reports always have abstracts, and review articles or term papers may or may not. Consider learning how to write one now, however, for two reasons.

First, you will eventually have to produce abstracts if you go on to publish material as a professional psychologist. APA journals require them for use by "indexing services," which list titles and abstracts of all journal articles published in a specific area during a year (*Psychological Abstracts* is an example). They are also used for many online databases, such as *PsycINFO*. Second, abstracts are so short (120 words or less) that they force you to synthesize your thinking into a cohesive and logical whole. If you can write a good abstract then the paper will flow more easily and all its parts will fit together smoothly.

Another important point about the Abstract is that it sets the tone for the balance of your message. This means that you should spend quality time constructing it. Be sure the Abstract accurately reflects the major points made in the paper. Omit the details but define all acronyms, abbreviations and esoteric terms that are unique to your topic. And be concise!

Introduction

The Introduction to a research report presents a question based on two components—a review of the literature and hypotheses that stem from that literature. It, therefore, provides a discussion of what research has previously addressed that question, and indicates the strategy to be used in obtaining an answer. A term paper generally cannot have an Introduction like this because there is no experiment being conducted. Instead, a term paper's focus is on a more detailed discussion of previous research in an area of interest, and on the writer's understanding and evaluation of that research. (There is no reason why an actual experiment could not be carried out for a term paper, but the extra steps involved in such an endeavor make it unusual.)

In a term paper, the Introduction portion of a "research report" is expanded to make up the main body of the paper. What kind of research has been done on the subject? Who has done this research? What were the findings and conclusions, and how do those findings compliment or contradict each other? Do *you* accept or doubt the findings? Why? Have previous researchers missed something? What areas of future research might be fruitful?

We must stress that when writing a term paper, or an Introduction to a research report, you are not basing the main points of the work on your *own* experiences. The primary purpose is to describe what is known about a topic based upon the research of others. Although you should constantly evaluate the information you are gaining from other researchers and are using to construct a term paper, your own opinions should be kept mostly for the conclusion section. Teachers who assign term papers *do* want to know your views on a topic, but they want those views to be informed ones, to be based upon a thorough understanding of what has been done previously.

Because a term paper primarily examines the work of other researchers, this is a good place to talk about "citing literature." When using the work of other scholars you *must* give them credit for their ideas and words. This is called "citing." Essentially, any "fact" included in a paper that you have not directly verified or which is not common knowledge must be accompanied by a citation. Thus, if you say "the sky is blue" you don't have to cite anyone for that. You can see it for yourself. But if you say that "the sky is blue because the short wavelengths of light are more easily scattered by air molecules in the upper atmosphere and those are the wavelengths that humans see as blue," then you need to tell the reader where you got that information. (An English physicist named John William Strutt, who was also known as Lord Rayleigh and who lived from 1842 to 1919, is generally credited for explaining this phenomenon.)

Deciding which facts are common knowledge and which aren't is not always easy. For example, writing that George Washington was the first president of the United States shouldn't have to be cited; everyone knows that. But what about the fact that Washington had a set of wooden dentures? If you wrote about Washington's wooden teeth without giving a citation for it, many people would accept it as common knowledge that didn't need to be cited, while others would exclaim: "I didn't know that!" The truth is, Washington never had wooden dentures; it may be common knowledge but it is actually a myth (Boller, 1996). Unless you are absolutely sure that something is common knowledge, err on the side of caution, double check your facts, and cite a reference.

Now, there are two *types* of citations in APA style, those that appear in the body of the paper itself, called "citations in text," and those that appear in the section called References. We'll talk about the latter when we get to that section, but for now let's look at citations in the body of the paper. These can be inserted in two ways: text citations and parenthetical citations. Either is appropriate.

A text citation might look like this: *Davis, Shaver, and Vernon (2003) found that attachment style was central to a partner's reaction to a relationship break up.* Note that the date appears in parentheses, but that the authors' names are used as the subject of the sentence. In a text citation the word "and" is used, but in a *parenthetical* citation the authors' names are included in the parentheses, and an ampersand (&) is used instead. Here's an example: *Attachment style appears to be central to a partner's reaction to a relationship break up (Davis, Shaver, & Vernon, 2003).* Each of these examples indicates that the "ideas" in the sentence belong to Davis, Shaver, and Vernon, but that the sentence itself is the work of the writer of this manuscript.

Occasionally, a writer might want to reproduce not only the ideas or findings of a previous manuscript, but also its wording. This is, of course, called quoting, and although quotes should be used sparingly they might be helpful if the original author's wording is especially apt. In APA style, citing quotes is very much like citing any other reference, except that you use quotation marks and include in the citation the page number of the work from which the quote was taken. For example: *Davis, Shaver, and Vernon (2003, p. 880) provides "the first demonstration of attachment-related reactions to breakups ranging from protest through coping to eventual resolution."* The quotation marks indicate *exactly* which words were taken from the other authors.

One more thing that you need to know about citing literature involves what to do in the case of multiple authors. If a piece has one or two authors, list that author or both authors in every citation. If, however, the piece has three, four, or five authors, then list all of them for the first citation (as in our recent Davis, Shaver and Vernon example), but in subsequent citations list only the first author followed by the Latin phrase "*et al.*" (which means "and others") and the date. Assuming that Davis, Shaver and Vernon had already been cited once in a paper, subsequent citations should appear as follows:

Davis et al. (2003) found that attachment style was central to a partner's reaction to a relationship break up.

Or

Attachment style appears to be central to a partner's reaction to a relationship break up (Davis et al., 2003).

For six or more authors, or for other variations such as a when a government agency is the "author" of a work, check the *Publication Manual* index under "reference citations." Also, always pay close attention to the way that the *Manual* says to space and punctuate citations. With *et al.*, for example, "*et*" does not have a period because it is a complete word (literally meaning "and" in Latin), but "*al.*" does have a period because it is an abbreviation for *alia*, which means "others" in Latin.

A term paper will typically have citations throughout—except in the conclusions, perhaps—but in a research report most citations will occur in the Introduction. In fact, many research report writers think of the Introduction as comprising two parts: a literature review and a statement of hypotheses. In either type of paper, the literature that is cited must be integrated in a way that makes a coherent point to the reader. This integration process will be examined more in coming chapters, but for now let's move on to a discussion of the remaining parts of a paper.

Method

The Method section is not found in a term paper except on those occasions when a student actually conducts an experiment and reports on it. In contrast, this section is crucial to a research report because it allows other scientists to: 1) see in a step-by-step fashion how a study was conducted, 2) evaluate the appropriateness of the method to the question(s) being asked, and 3) repeat (replicate) the study themselves if they wish.

Where Method sections appear they are usually divided into subsections on "participants" (the people or animals who act as subjects in a study), and on "procedure" (a step by step, day by day account of what happened to the participants). Subsections such as "apparatus" (equipment) or "analysis" (statistics used) may occasionally be added. The important point is to give the details of what was done, how it was done, and why.

Results

As with methods, a term paper does not have a Results *section* unless that paper is a report of an actual experiment. If data *have* been collected, then they are summarized in the Results, usually in statistical form. Seldom are a study participant's individual scores found, though. Rather, there will be means and standard deviations taken from groups of scores, and most probably the significance levels of statistical tests like the Analysis of Variance. There are likely to be some written statements indicating the specific results, but without much discussion about what those results might mean. Term papers may summarize results from a number of research studies but will generally do so in words rather than numbers, and this should be integrated with the rest of the text, not shoehorned into a separate section.

If your paper *is* proposing a research study or reporting obtained results, however, then you need to know both how to select an appropriate statistic to use for analysis, *and* how to report those statistics in written form. If you haven't had a statistics or research methods course then this probably sounds difficult, but those courses and some practice will help the process become "second nature."

The "process" of reporting results is the same for any analysis. That is, usually, the author reports the statistical symbol, followed by the degrees of freedom (in parentheses), the obtained value of the statistic, and the probability value of the statistic. A t-test may appear as follows, for example: $t (18) = 3.46, p < .05$. Likewise, an author may report a correlation coefficient as: $r (28) = -.65, p < .05$.

Note the similar way in which these analyses are reported. Such statistical statements will be accompanied by *some* explanatory text, but not much. The explanations and interpretations will come in the Discussion section.

Discussion

It is in the Discussion section of a research paper that scientists get to tell their readers what their results mean. A brief summary of the major results is usually given, and then some interpretations are made. Were the results as expected? If so, what does that mean? What if the results were not as expected? Is there a possible explanation? Are there any implications for current theories in the field?

This section gives the researcher some leeway to draw conclusions and to speculate. The Discussion also allows the researcher to show critical thought by considering alternative explanations (from those hypothesized) for the obtained results. Finally, the researcher should use this space to point out limitations of the study (no study is problem-free) and potential directions for future research. By indicating an awareness of the weaknesses or short-comings of a study, and by giving other researchers suggestions for continuing the line of literature, an author demonstrates humility and an awareness that science is an ongoing process.

The discussion portion of a *term paper* is usually not isolated from the body of the text, although sometimes there will be a separate piece at the end called "Conclusions." Instead, the term paper as a whole consists of paragraphs that introduce and define the topic, paragraphs that describe previous research and current thinking about the topic, and paragraphs that give the writer's opinions and conclusions.

(Note: For *research reports*, think of them as being shaped like an hourglass. The Introduction should start broad, with a statement of the general problem up for investigation, and then narrow down toward the more specific topics. The Method and Results will be quite focused, as they refer only to the study at hand. The Discussion, however, will start narrow, recapping the study being reported or proposed, and become more broad as implications and future directions are considered.)

References

References are just as important to a term paper as they are to a research report. A good References section ensures that the people whose work you used in writing a paper are properly credited. It also makes life easier for other researchers and writers who want to read your informational sources for themselves.

For example, if Alan Smith and Inez Jones were the people who developed a theory that you discuss in a paper, then they deserve credit for being first. And if reading your paper makes me want to read Smith and Jones, then you should make it easy for me to find their work by giving me the who, what, and where. This is part of the courtesy that scholarly writers extend to their readers, and it is an important element in helping to advance human knowledge. Each specific reference should have the name(s) of the author(s), the title of the article or book, the place where the article or book was published, and the publication date. References to journal articles also include page numbers.

Although most style manuals agree on *what* should be included in a reference, they part company on *how*. APA style is very specific, and though some of the rules seem arbitrary (and are) it is important to follow them. For a term paper, at least part of your grade is likely to depend on the correct use of APA style. The reason teachers do this is because they know that the journals to which you will later submit as a professional—and we expect everyone to become a professional—will expect material to be submitted in the proper format. In fact, those journals will not even bother to read material that is improperly prepared.

A good way to develop a feel for the APA's references style is to see a picture. The *Publication Manual* provides one in that sample paper we mentioned in our section on "Title Page." (In the 5th edition of the *Manual*, this begins on page 313.) Looking at that sample will show that all references are double spaced and alphabetized, and that the first line of each reference is flush-left, with the rest of the lines indented. This is called a *hanging-indent*. A brief illustration of the references format follows here:

Brookover, B. C. (2005). *Psychology and aging in urban environments*. New Orleans, LA: Lanoue Publications.
Hammer, E. D., & Gramlich, C. A. (2004). *Psychology*

made easier (Rev. ed.). Denver, CO: DuBois Press.

Hammer, E. D., & Irvin, Y. (2007). Colons: Their proper use in psychological writing. *Journal of Scholarly Punctuation, 19*, 125-132.

Rider, D. P., & Gipson, L. J. (2002). The psychology student as a metaphor for America. *Xavier's Journal of Advanced Literacy Theory, 240*, 111-112.

Valentine, G. M. (2007, November). *Hurricane Katrina and me: One woman's personal odyssey.* Paper presented at the meeting of the Global Warming Association, Abita Springs, LA.

The first two references here are for books, the next two for journal articles, and the last one to a paper presented at a conference but not yet published in print. (These are all made up, by the way.) As you can see, there are similarities and differences among the three types of references. Titles of books and presentations are italicized, for example, while titles of articles are not. Titles of *journals* are italicized, though.

You may also have references to abstracts, newspapers, unpublished dissertation research, the internet, or even TV shows. Each of these has its own peculiar requirements, and you'll be able to find out how to write just about any kind of reference in the *Publication Manual*, which has a chapter devoted to the topic. For specific questions, check the *Manual's* Index under "Reference Citations" or "Reference List."

All references, except personal communications and those primary sources that you couldn't find and where you had to rely on a "secondary source," must appear in the text as well as in the reference list. Personal communications are bits of information that are told to you in interviews, phone conversations, or in personal letters and memos, but are not published in a public and formal way. Suppose a professor named Stripling tells you in his office that, "the Garcia Effect is another name for conditioned flavor aversion," and you want to use this fact in a paper but can't find it written down anywhere. Well, cite it in the text of the paper as a personal communication, with the following format: (J. S. Stripling, personal communication, October 14, 2007). Because there is no written publication to cite, this would appear *only* in the body of the paper and not in the References list. Personal emails should be cited in this same way.

Secondary sources are those in which you read about facts discovered by yet *other* researchers. The "primary source" is the original work, where the information *first* appeared. Say you're reading a work on evolution by Richard Hawkins and he makes some claims about what Charles Darwin said in the book, *On the Origin of Species*. If you use the material that *Hawkins* credits to Charles Darwin in a paper, then you're using a secondary source. Darwin would be the primary source.

Always make every effort to use original sources, but if you simply cannot physically obtain that work, you *can* use secondary sources as long as they are clearly indicated as such. The text citation for a secondary source would look like: "Darwin (as cited in Hawkins, 1999), argued that...." Only Hawkins would appear in the References *list*, however, because you never actually read Darwin. In our experience, many students use secondary sources in their papers without being aware of it. Be careful about this because, if Hawkins got Darwin wrong and you use the same information without letting us know that it came from Hawkins, then it looks like *you* are the one who got Darwin wrong.

Finally, a few words should be said concerning information cited from the Internet. We will talk much more about the strengths and dangers of the internet in Chapter 4, but be aware that many of today's scientific journals provide some or all of their content "online" as electronic media. Although readers should be cautious and skeptical about much of what they read online, there is no reason why internet sources such as government documents or electronic components of established print journals cannot be used as references. The *Publication Manual* gives examples of how to cite such documents and periodicals. See the *Manual*'s index under "electronic sources."

Appendix

In a book or a long research article, an Appendix is a great way to present detailed information that would disrupt the flow of the text if placed in the body of the paper. For example, in a work discussing phobias you wouldn't want to stop after the first paragraph and list all the different kinds of phobias (there are well over a hundred). This kind of information would fit better in an Appendix. Few term papers need an Appendix, although there is no particular reason *not* to use one. See the *Publication Manual* for details, but typically an Appendix will be placed on a separate sheet at the end of a paper, with the label "Appendix" at the top.

Tables and Figures

Tables are used in research reports to present and summarize numerical data, such as means, standard deviations, and significance levels. Figures are pictures—like graphs, drawings, or photos. They may present numerical data, as in a graph, but they could also show illustrative examples of a phenomenon, such as a drawing made by a person with a certain type of brain damage. In a published article, tables and figures are found within the Results section. However, in a manuscript submitted for publication, or for a grade in a class, the tables and figures are on separate sheets at the end of a paper. See the *Publication Man-*

ual's index under "tables" and "figures" for the page numbers in the *Manual* where these topics are discussed.

Term papers can probably benefit from tables and figures, though it would be best to use them sparingly. For example, if your paper is on the types of schizophrenia then it might be helpful for the reader to have a table that lists the basic types and their characteristic symptoms. This is certainly not a requirement, however. Be aware that if you use figures or tables that you didn't produce yourself then you will need citations and may well need to request *permission* from the originator of the material. Figures and tables from published material are typically copyrighted to the creator and reproducing copyrighted material without permission is illegal.

When copying a figure just for a term paper, however, you can generally claim "Fair use." Fair use is when material is reproduced primarily for educational purposes and not for professional reasons or to earn money. You could not use a copyrighted figure in work intended for publication, for example, unless you had permission.

Footnotes and Author Notes

There are various ways to put extra explanatory information into a text without disrupting a paper's flow. Footnotes and author notes are two ways, and both are described in the *Publication Manual*. Author notes, for example, tell the reader information about the writer of a paper, how they can be contacted or how their research was funded. Neither footnotes nor author notes are really needed in a term paper.

Conclusions

No chapter on APA style in any guidebook can replace the need to study the *Publication Manual*. That doesn't mean you have to memorize it, but be familiar enough with it to know what is available in the *Manual* and where to look within it for the answers to questions about style, content, and the presentation of a manuscript or term paper. Know that journals do not necessarily conform to APA style when they *publish* articles. Nevertheless, even the most renowned psychologists must abide by the same rules that you do when they *submit* articles to a journal. Consider a term paper as practice for such a submission and *check that APA style.*

CHAPTER THREE

SELECTING IDEAS

"I'm a writer as rarely as possible, when forced by an idea too lovely to let die unwritten."
—Richard Bach

If done well, a research paper forms a coherent, organized whole. The paragraphs flow smoothly from one to the other, and the facts that support the paper's conclusions are readily apparent. What many new writers do not realize is that the coherence and completeness is the product of many different steps and much hard work. In this chapter, we'll talk first about the initial step involved in constructing a good "term paper," selecting an appropriate idea or topic.

In Chapter 1 we suggested choosing something interesting to write about in your term paper. In fact, let your sense of what is interesting be your guide all through the development and completion of the work. So, where do interesting ideas come from? If you pay attention, they're everywhere. They're found in newspapers, books, TV shows, and in conversations with friends. For papers assigned in a particular course, pay special attention to interesting things that your classroom teacher says, or that are found in your textbook. Ask yourself, what have I heard, read, or seen that I'd like to know more about. *That's* the kind of topic to select.

Having chosen an exciting topic, however, does not mean you are finished with the job of selecting an idea. Many other things still have to be done. We'll call this process "refining," and the first step in refining an idea is to find out whether there is enough information available in the form of books, articles, or experts, to allow you to complete a paper of a given length on the topic in question. In other words, will there be enough facts available to fill a paper of, say, ten pages, given that some of those pages will have to be used for your own thoughts and interpretations?

The answer to the above question depends on both the quality of the library and other available sources, and on how specific or broad the topic is that you've chosen. Library quality will be discussed in Chapter 4, but it is generally of less importance than the nature of a topic. For example, no library or internet web page will be able to help much for a subject like "What We Know about the Surface of Jupiter." On the other hand, almost any college library will provide hundreds, if not thousands, of articles and books on a topic like "Mental Disorders." (Note: no matter how big your library is, it might be wise to select a topic different from that chosen by others in your class. Otherwise you'll be competing for references and they might check out a book that you need.)

Choosing the surface of Jupiter as a topic is a bad idea because almost nothing is known about the subject. Scientists doubt that Jupiter even has a surface in the normal usage of the word (Pasachoff, 1987). The mental disorder example is almost as bad, however, because so much information is available that the topic could never be covered adequately in a typical term paper. The key word is *almost*, since it *is* easier to leave out known information than it is to discover sources that do not exist.

If you choose a "broad" topic like "Mental Disorders" then a huge amount of material will certainly have to be left out. A ten page term paper might provide just enough room to list all the disorders but it would not leave much space for discussing them. Deciding what material to leave out is part of the process of refining. It is often referred to as "narrowing your idea."

Narrowing an idea first involves identifying the sub-topics that make up the broader category. An obvious example would be to list the various mental disorders—such as depression, conversion disorder, and schizophrenia—and then select *one* of them to write about. Most disorders could probably be covered in ten pages, though it would be difficult to discuss much more than generalities. With schizophrenia, for example, there might be room to talk about the history of the disorder, to cover the types and their symptoms, and perhaps to add a few paragraphs on one or two major theories about causes. There would not be room to go into detail on any particular issue, or to illustrate the paper with a large number of case studies. Schizophrenia is still a pretty broad topic.

A question to ask about now is: "How do they (meaning your authors) know which topics are broad and which are narrow?" The answer is, through experience. We know because we have read widely in our areas, and because we've written papers ourselves that varied in length and attention to detail. The only way for *you* to start gaining this experience is by digging into the literature in your field. Just as you set aside time for studying and for writing, set aside time each week to read books and articles on psychology. This is going to be your career, after all.

Spending time in the library looking at what has been published in the field will give you an idea about the resources available on a variety of issues. Until then, however, take a glance through the lists that follow. They may suggest some rules for judging the broadness or narrowness of a topic.

Broad Topics: (General; large amounts of information from many sources, introductory texts, journals, monographs, manuals.)

1. The Mental Disorders.
2. The Historical Schools of Psychology.
3. The Parts of the Brain and Their Function.
4. The History of Psychoanalysis.
5. The Sensory Systems of the Brain and How They Work.
6. A Comparison of the Personality Theories of Freud, Adler, Jung, Skinner, and Allport.

Narrow Topics: (Information is located in journals, texts, or monographs written at a more specific level, in physiology for example.)

1. How Brain Cells Talk to Each Other.
2. How the Eye Works.
3. The Steps Involved in Systematic Desensitization.
4. The Life of B.F. Skinner.
5. Anorexia Nervosa.
6. Schizophrenia.
7. How to Carry out a Simple Experiment.
8. The Freudian Defense Mechanisms.
9. An Outline of Brain Anatomy.
10. Freud's Psychosexual Stages.
11. A Brief description of the Major Psychological Methods.
12. Piaget's Stages of Cognitive Development.

Probably none of the "Broad Topics" could be dealt with successfully in a ten-to-fifteen-page term paper. All of the "Narrow Topics" could be covered, though some would have to be handled in a general fashion without much detailed discussion. It seems unlikely, however, that many of the narrow topics could be crammed into a five page paper. For five pages look at such issues as:

1. The Definition of Psychology and How it has Changed Historically.
2. The Parts of a Neuron, With a Discussion of Their Function.
3. The Early Life of B. F. Skinner.
4. The Freudian Concept of the Id.
5. The Defense Mechanism of Repression.
6. The Difference between Positive and Negative Reinforcement.

You might think it would be hard to write five pages on the definition of psychology and how it has changed over the last hundred years or so, but that just means you don't know quite enough psychology yet. The length of a paper is, in large part, a function of how much detail is included. All you have to do to write five pages on changes in the definition of psychology is to add some detail about the people who developed the definitions and the times in which they lived.

As an exercise for this section of the book, develop two lists of characteristics. The first list should include the characteristics of your hand; the second list should include the characteristics of a human being. The second list will be much longer than the first and certainly seems to provide more information for a paper. Just describing all the parts would take up many pages. In contrast, the hand list has only a few items on it, and they don't fill up much space.

You're right, of course, in thinking that the "human being" list provides more material for a paper, but you are wrong in believing the "hand" list is short. Look at your hand again, and this time notice all the details you missed the first time. Did you mention that the skin feels slightly different on the palm than on the back? Did you mention cuts or scars? Did you indicate whether your fingernails are long or short, or whether they have any blemishes? Did you count the number of whorls in each fingerprint? Did you measure your lifeline? As you can see, the length of a list depends upon the details. The same is true for a paper.

Now, let's continue our discussion on refining ideas by looking at a sample from the "narrow" topics mentioned above. Any of these would be suitable for a ten to fifteen page paper, but let's pick anorexia nervosa, a popular choice among students. (Please keep this example in mind because we'll return to it in Chapter 4.) Our next step in refining is to determine our "direction of approach." With anorexia, we'll have to decide whether to discuss it from a biological, psychological, or sociological perspective. Each approach is valid but a ten to fifteen page term paper is too short to deal with all three.

Even assigned topics usually leave room for choosing a theoretical approach. It might be between pro and con, or between historical analysis and current analysis. Try to make this decision as soon as possible after selecting a topic, however, since it will help save time once you begin searching out the major sources for the paper. Do remember, though, that just because you start out looking at anorexia from a biological point of view does not mean necessarily that you have to end that way (bearing in mind the instructor's demands for the class). Change the approach if you really want to, but be aware that this will require going back and rethinking some earlier decisions about the paper.

Once you've decided how to approach a paper, a good strategy might be to sit down and write notes on what you already know about the topic. Maybe you know that the term anorexia means "no appetite," or maybe you remember a teacher saying the disorder is most likely to strike young women. Put those details down and keep them in mind while searching for more material. It is important to try and connect new information to already known information.

At this point, we suggest you get organized about gathering the facts for your paper. Buy some folders and label one of them in bright red ink: "Anorexia Nervosa Term Paper." Put all your notes on anorexia into that folder, and set aside a space in your room to store it. If you have other term paper projects, make a separate folder for each. And hang on to those folders after the work is finished. Research is never wasted and you might just want that information again in a few years.

We are now to a point, though, where we cannot move further without digging deeply into the information needed to actually write a term paper. This includes using the internet, but not *just* the internet. At some point you'll need to venture into the library and look at some actual books and journals. So, grab your folder, find a handy pen and some notepaper, and let's begin our hunt for information. The next chapter will take us there.

CHAPTER FOUR

FINDING SOURCES/ USING THE INTERNET AND LIBRARY

"...research is never completed.... Around the corner lurks another possibility of interview, another book to read, a courthouse to explore, a document to verify."
—Catherine Drinker Bowen

Although you may know *some* information about a topic like anorexia before choosing it, to do a good job on a term paper you'll need to do extensive background reading on the subject. Why? Because you simply will not know enough to write with confidence about the topic. The place to start this reading is with a textbook, a place to continue it is on the internet, and the place to finish it is in a library.

This chapter deals with the process involved in finding the sources needed to become an expert, at least a partial expert, on the topic of your paper. We'll start with the internet, where many students start, but will spend the bulk of this chapter talking about the library. We also want to say some things about picking good sources from bad, and about textbooks, which can serve as personal extensions of the library. Classroom texts provide "start-up" information on many topics and can help map out where more detail is needed. For these reasons, it is probably best to pick a topic from the text for your class. This is a suggestion, not a rule, but it *will* help ease the writing burden if you follow it. You won't be able to depend solely on a text, however. It won't have enough information. Fleshing out the knowledge skeleton provided by the text will require exploring other sources.

The Internet

Most of today's students probably begin their search for information for a paper on the internet. Unfortunately, many of them end there as well. The internet is a marvelous tool, but it's not always the *best* tool for researchers to use. And sometimes it can cause more problems than it solves.

For example, say you are doing that paper on anorexia nervosa. You hop on Wikipedia for a definition and description, jot down that information in a computer file for your paper, and you're off and running. Sorry, but you've just made a mistake. Wikipedia is a fun place to browse, but do you realize that essentially *anyone* can change an entry on Wikipedia if they don't like it? Entries are changed constantly, sometimes by experts, sometimes by people with axes to grind, and sometimes by people who just want to mess with other folk's heads. For a formal paper, *never* use a definition from Wikipedia without double checking it against some published print source like a textbook. Better yet, save time and go to the textbook first.

OK, skip Wikipedia, you say. Just "Google" anorexia. Here's what the authors of this *Guidebook* came up with when we did that. The first two links were to treatment centers that specialize in eating disorders. In other words, they make money from treating people with such disorders. We're sure the folks at both centers are well-intentioned, but they are in the business of selling their services. They are not objective scholars. The third link was to womenshealth.gov. The "gov" means that this information comes from a government agency, and it is certainly worth a look. Who wrote it, however? Was he or she an expert in the field? We don't know. There are links to other government websites, but no mention of the specific researchers who prepared the material. Government sites are often pretty good, but they are generally not the *best* sites to use.

Moving on, our fourth link was to Wikipedia, but the fifth link was to a site on mental health that encourages people to "diagnose themselves," always a risky business. Finally, eight links down we find an article by a real person, Tracy A. Farkas, MD., whose affiliations are listed on the site. Here we are even given the names of an editorial board, names of people who are responsible for checking the accuracy of Dr. Farkas's work. This is not a *guarantee* of accuracy, but if Dr. Farkas has said something wrong then she has opened herself publicly to criticism, as has each board member who failed to catch the errors. Reputations are at stake, and that makes it likely that the information is as accurate as these authors can possibly make it. Thus, the eighth link down is the first one to start with in researching information for your paper, but would all students have had the patience to get there?

Another point about information discovered through general online searches is that most websites you visit will have exactly the same basic information. This is good in that consensus tends to suggest accuracy, and when using the internet *always* check multiple sources to see if they agree. However, the consensus also means that the more links clicked the less *new* information received. Will there be enough to complete a ten page paper?

One thing to do to improve the quality of an internet search is to go to Google's "advanced search" option, scroll down to "Topic-Specific Searches," and click on "Google Scholar." This time most of the links will be to actual research reports written for scholarly journals and will include the authors' names and affiliations. However, be aware that you may have to register at some sites before accessing full articles, and there may be a fee attached. Also, since most of this material is uploaded from journal archives, it will often be weighted toward older articles. Our Google Scholar search on Anorexia turned up dates like 1979, 1980, 1987, 1991. The newest stuff is in the newest journals, which are in libraries or accessible through libraries.

The internet is handy and contains much that is good. It also contains a lot of information that is inaccurate, and sometimes it has material that is deliberately misstated. There is no reason why good material can't be found for your paper on the net, but be aware of two things. First, do not depend solely on the internet. The newest and best material either won't be there or won't be available to you for free access. (We'll tell you a way around this problem when we get to libraries.) Second, when using the net, be aware that search engines like Google do *not* sort entries by the accuracy of the material or by relevance to your paper. Very often, the first few links that show up will be more commercially than scholarly oriented. Even more than with printed sources, the internet requires that you apply all your critical faculties to determine what to pay attention to and what to ignore.

The Library

Libraries can be intimidating places to look for information. You just want a few books on a specific topic, but how are you going to find them among the thousands nestled on the shelves? The situation isn't much better when looking for journal articles. Psychology is a rapidly growing field and new findings appear daily. Of course, most libraries will get only a fraction of all the material that is published, but even the total mass of *available* material can easily be daunting. And modern technology has increased the amount of accessible information by a huge margin.

Because of all the books, journals, newspapers, and magazines available, if you don't enter a library with some knowledge about how to locate information then you can hunt for hours without finding a single reference to a specific topic. As an example, one of your authors was in the library a few years ago when a student came up to say that she couldn't locate anything about anorexia nervosa. (See why we picked anorexia as our example in Chapter 3?) Within about five minutes the faculty member found seven books referring to that topic. This doesn't mean the student was dumb and the faculty member smart. It means the faculty member knew from experience where and how to look. Consider the three steps that follow and you'll be on the way to knowing those same things.

Step 1. *Using a Textbook to Help Locate Sources*

Odd as it seems, the *first* place to look for library sources is in the textbooks for your classes. All textbooks, including this one, contain an "index," sometimes specifically called a "subject index." Most other scientific books do as well. The index is organized alphabetically and gives the page numbers where a certain topic is discussed within the work. If you want to know whether a book has something in it about anorexia nervosa, for example, then check the subject index. What follows is a sample of the kind of entries that might be seen; it's taken from an actual text, *Abnormal Psychology*, by Meyer and Salmon (1988),

which we are going to use here for demonstration purposes
only.

    Angular gyrus, 491, 497
    Animals, fear of, 214
    Anorexia nervosa, 588, 596
      parents of, 597
      treatment, 598
    Anoxia, 251

In this book, anorexia nervosa is discussed on pages 588 and 596. The parents of anorexia sufferers are mentioned on page 597, and treatments are described on 598. These are the pages to read for the information you want.

A textbook can help even more, however. It can identify the first sources you need from the library. How? Well, let's use the anorexia example to demonstrate. First, the subject index of *Abnormal Psychology* tells us what pages to look at for anorexia. When we go read those pages we find "citations in text," which we talked about in Chapter 2 and which are part of APA style. These represent sources of information that Meyer and Salmon used in developing their discussion of anorexia. All psychology texts have such citations. In fact, all scholarly books have something similar, though it might be in the form of footnotes or endnotes.

On page 596 of Meyer and Salmon (1988) we find the following citation in text: (Abraham and Jones, 1984). This means Abraham and Jones wrote a piece in 1984 that dealt with anorexia, and Meyer and Salmon read this piece and used it to help *them* write about the disorder. A little further on in *Abnormal Psychology* we find mention of (Agras, 1987), and (Bruch, 1986). These are two more works that Meyer and Salmon used in writing their piece on anorexia. Presumably, Meyer and Salmon know more about anorexia than you do, and they must have learned most of what they know from the sources they used in writing their book. Why not use their sources to help *you* write a paper on the disorder? Your textbook will help locate them.

In addition to a subject index and citations in text, all textbooks, and most other scholarly books, will also contain a "References" section. In *Abnormal Psychology* this starts at the back of the book with page R-1. It's arranged in alphabetical order by author, and it contains a complete reference, which means that it gives the title of the article, the names of the people who wrote it, and where and when the article appeared. As an exercise, let's trace Abraham and Jones (1984), which we pointed out previously as a citation in text. We first turn to the References section of Meyer and Salmon, and we see that Abraham and Jones (1984) is right there on the first page we look at. The reference reads:

Abraham, S., & Jones, D. (1984). *Eating disorders*. New York: Oxford University Press.

Eating Disorders is italicized in the textbook, just as it is written here. If *Eating Disorders* was a journal then there would also be an article title listed. Since this is not the case, we know that *Eating Disorders* is a book. We also know that it was published in New York in 1984 by Oxford University Press.

A little later in this chapter we'll follow-up by going to the library to try and find *Eating Disorders*, but for now let's look at another example, (Bruch, 1986), which we also saw as a citation in text. We turn to the references in Meyer and Salmon and look for the "B's." Bruch (1986) is on page R-5, and the reference reads:

Bruch, H. (1986). Anorexia nervosa: The therapeutic task. In K. Brownell and J. Foreyt (Eds.) *Handbook of Eating Disorders*. New York: Basic Books.

This tells us that Bruch's article is called "Anorexia nervosa: The therapeutic task," and that it appears in a book called the *Handbook of Eating Disorders*, which was published in New York by Basic Books. It also shows that the book is a collection of articles edited by K. Brownell and J. Foreyt. (The use of initials instead of first names is common in scientific journals because it saves space, which is important to many publishers.)

Although both references we looked up were to books, most references will probably be to journals, which are generally the first places new research gets published. Books pull together information from a wide range of sources but are usually not reporting research for the first time. A rule of thumb is that anything in a textbook is probably at least two or three years old. When writing a paper in a rapidly changing field, psychology or computer science for example, then some of what you read in your text is already out of date. For this reason, use journals whenever possible. In psychology, except for historical purposes, or to illustrate a point as we are doing here, it's probably not a good idea to use articles more than eight or ten years old, and few books more than five or six years old.

Step 2. Choosing Good References Instead of Bad

While on the topic of references to use or not to use, let's make a few more comments on "good" and "bad" sources for a paper. Most references should be to books or journals, with journals being the better of the two. Journals are not only more current, but they are also peer-reviewed, which means that every article in them has been checked by at least a couple of other researchers who are considered experts on the subject in question. Books, on the other hand, *can* be great, but their information may be years old, and sometimes their publication rests more on their likelihood of generating sales than on their empirical value. There are, however, some sources that should not be used for a paper, or, at best, should be used only sparingly. These are:

a. *Dictionaries*: Dictionaries are important writing tools but are not good research sources because they are too generic, too general. When looking for a definition of anorexia nervosa, use a textbook definition, not a dictionary one.

b. *Encyclopedias*: Encyclopedias are great sources of background material and make for interesting reading, but they are usually not specific enough to use as references in a term paper. Textbooks, monographs, and journals have the detail that is needed.

c. *Newspapers*: Use newspapers only for teaser items, for anecdotes or quotes. If you discover an interesting article in the paper, then follow-up by looking into the original source. Many newspapers *do* report on where their information comes from. Part of the reason for being careful is that newspapers can be inaccurate when it comes to scientific matters, mainly because journalists are not trained scientists and often lack a deep understanding of the research area they are covering.

d. *Popular Magazines*: Use magazines like *Time Magazine* and *Newsweek* only in the same way as newspapers, for anecdotes and quotes. It's not necessarily that they are inaccurate, because their staff reporters and freelancers have more time to research articles and are usually better informed than the average newspaper reporter, but magazines often do not have the kind of objectivity and detail that is needed.

Remember that newspapers and magazines survive by selling subscriptions and advertisements. They need to popularize their content, and sometimes sensationalize it, to attract readers. Journals, on the other hand, are usually supported by government agencies or universities. They don't sell subscriptions to survive and their major claim to fame is the unbiased accuracy of the research they report.

e. *Popular Books*: The "do not use except for anecdotes" rule is not as clear for popular books as it is for popular magazines and newspapers. Many popular books are written by good scientists who have a knack for simplifying the language of their field. Such writers include Stephen J. Gould, Lewis Thomas, and Carl Sagan. Books by authors such as these can be used as sources, though they are often heavy on examples and weak on details. Other popular books, however, are written by quacks, and they will do far more harm than good.

Unfortunately, it's not always easy to tell good science from quackery. One of your authors remembers as a young teen discovering a "non-fiction" book that seemed to prove that alien beings had visited earth in the ancient past and influenced our history. It was a couple of years before that teenager had read enough *real* science to understand that the "non-fiction" book was actually a thin gruel of half-baked truths, outright lies, and wild speculations. It was infuriating.

How can you protect yourself from being fooled in this way? There are two ways of doing so. First, learn as much as possible about how science really works and what scientists really know. Second, cultivate a healthy sense of skepticism. Always ask how people learned the things they tell you. Did they see it themselves? Did the cousin of somebody's cousin tell them about it? Did they read it somewhere, and, if so, where? Would you believe it if they said they read it in the *New York Times*? What if they said it was in the *National Enquirer*?

Many books and articles are published each year on subjects like ESP, UFOs, ghosts, Bigfoot, and the Loch Ness Monster. There is nothing to say that these phenomena *cannot* exist. They can even be great fun to speculate about and they often make for wonderful stories and movies. But that is just where they should generally be kept, in casual conversation, or in movies and novels. There is no clear scientific evidence for the existence of these phenomena. There is only speculation, and in science speculation must be clearly labeled as such. Any written work that claims to *prove* the existence of these kinds of phenomena should be read with caution and skepticism. The more outrageous the claim, the more proof you should demand before accepting it. (For an excellent book on the subject of scientific skepticism see Michael Shermer's *Why People Believe Weird Things*.")

Step 3. Finding Sources in the Library

Now that we've discussed sources to use or not to use, let's take some of the citations in text that we mentioned earlier in this chapter and explore the library to see if we can find them. Specifically, let's look for the two sources in Meyer and Salmon's *Abnormal Psychology* (1988) that we located from the subject index of that book. Remember that these were Abraham and Jones (1984), and Bruch (1986).

Libraries used to have "card catalogs," which would be a series of filing cabinets with individually typed 3 x 5 cards listing every book and author on that library's shelves. Can you imagine how much hassle that was? Modern libraries store their holdings on computer instead, in what is called an electronic or "online" catalog, and if you have access to the internet you probably won't even have to physically enter a library to find out if it has a specific book.

Whether searching a public library or a university one, whether from a personal computer or from a terminal in the library building itself, all electronic catalogs are pretty much the same. At Xavier University of Louisiana, where most of your authors are located, this computerized storehouse is called XAC (Xavier Automated Catalog). We'll use XAC as a model for discussion, but the information presented here should transfer easily to any university system.

Both the references we want are books, so let's pretend we're sitting down in a library, or all comfortable in front of our computer, to find them. (We'll consider how to find journals later.) Locate the library's main web page and click on the "catalog" link. Online catalogs are organized in three primary ways, by author, title, and subject, although most will allow other, less common, ways of searching as well. One reference we want is Abraham and Jones (1984). Abraham seems a good place to start. We know from the Reference section of *Abnormal Psychology* that Abraham's first name begins with "S." To find out if our library has a book by this writer, we select "author" search and enter the name we want to find. This means typing "last name first name" (e.g., Abraham S) and clicking on the search button.

What comes up on our screen is a listing of those authors with last names alphabetically close to Abraham who have books in the library, including Abraham S we hope. In this case, in XAC, our hope is fulfilled. Abraham S (S is for Suzanne) shows on the screen with a number next to the name indicating that there are two of her books in the library. We now select and click the line where Abraham S appears, and this brings up a second screen showing the titles and call numbers of those books, as well as such information as the publishers and publication date. *Eating Disorders*, the book we're looking for, is one of the two.

We could have found this same book in three other ways. We could have done an author search by "Jones D," Abraham's co-author. We could have searched directly by title, in which case we would have selected "title search" and typed in "Eating Disorders." Or, finally, we could have started by looking for books on the topic we were interested in. This is called a "subject search" and is much less efficient than searching by author or title. To do one we select "subject search" and type in our keywords (e.g., eating disorders).

Subject searches may help if more specific information isn't available on a source, but they are hit or miss operations. A subject search using "anorexia" as the keyword might not turn up a book called *Eating Disorders*. And a search for "eating disorders" might get information on obesity or bulimia rather than anorexia. Still, unless you know the authors or titles that you want, a subject search may be a necessity, and it *can* help expand a collection of references. Just make sure to search for material on a topic using all the keywords you can think of.

The most important information provided by a search like the one we've just done is the "call number." For *Eating Disorders*, this is 616.852 A159e. This is a code to help locate a specific book among other volumes in the library. Each book has a different code and everything is in numerical or alphabetical order—616.852 A159e comes after 616.1 A159e and before 617.1 A159e. For this exercise, your authors went looking on the shelves of the Xavier library and found *Eating Disorders* exactly where it was supposed to be. (Note: People browsing a library's shelves can easily put books back in the wrong order, so if you can't find your source try reading titles to the left and right, on the shelves above and below, or even on the opposite side of the aisle because people sometimes turn around as they're looking at a book and then stuff it back in the first hole they find among the other volumes.)

Now that we've found one source, let's look for our other reference—Bruch (1986). Remember that this was an article that appeared in a collection edited by K. Brownell and J. Foreyt entitled *Handbook of Eating Disorders*. We can look under the book's title, or under either Brownell or Foreyt, but, unfortunately, there is no listing for this book, which means Xavier's library doesn't have it. "Forget about it," you say? And hope you don't need it? Not necessarily. If you want it, there is a way to get it. It's called interlibrary loan.

Interlibrary loan allows students access to a book or journal that their library does not own. It's simple. Just go to the library and request an "Interlibrary Loan Form," or, even easier, go to the library's homepage and fill out one online. These forms differ from university to university, but most will have a place for your name, department, and status (i.e., faculty or student). They'll also ask for information about the book or article that you want, such as author, title, publisher, page numbers, and so on. Most or all of this information can be found in the original reference used to identify the book or article, the reference section of Meyer and Salmon's (1988) *Abnormal Psychology*, for example, which is where we got the name Bruch.

In Bruch's case you probably want to request the whole text within which his or her article appears. After all, a book called the *Handbook of Eating Disorders* might have considerable information for a paper on anorexia nervosa, and, at worst, it would let you read about the problem of anorexia within the context of other eating disturbances.

Once the form is completed, turn it over to the librarian and wait. The librarian sends the request to a university that has the book or article, and it will arrive at *your* library anywhere from a few days to a few weeks after the request is made, depending on the university from which it is being borrowed. This means you have to plan ahead to use interlibrary loan. If you wait until the last minute to start working on a paper then a requested reference may not arrive before it's time for the final draft to be handed in. Occasionally, there is a cost attached to interlibrary loan, usually for photocopying an article, but the service is basically free. Books are checked out like any other book and can be renewed. Photocopies are yours to keep.

We have now located one book in the library and put in an interlibrary request for another. We've not yet looked for journal articles so let's turn to that process next.

To start, let's go back to *Abnormal Psychology* by Meyer and Salmon (1988), which is where we found citations to Abraham and Jones (1984) and Bruch (1986). (Remember that we're using this book for demonstration purposes; you'll want more recent sources for *your* paper.) There are several more references mentioned in the eating disorder section of *Abnormal Psychology*. Two are: Fallon and Rozin (1985), and Polivy and Herman (1985). When we look in the References section of the book we find that both of these are journal articles. The full references are:

Fallon, A., & Rozin, P. (1985). Sex differences in perceptions of desirable body shape. *Journal of Abnormal Psychology, 94,* 102-105.

Polivy, J., & Herman, C. (1985). Dieting and binging. *American Psychologist, 40,* 193-201.

These references provide all the information needed to locate the articles in question. They give author, year, title, name of the journal, and the volume and page numbers (e.g., Volume 94, pages 102 through 105). The first step is to see if your library has the journals or if interlibrary loan is called for again. You can find out by turning once more to the online catalog. For example, on XAC (Xavier's online catalog) and most other university library catalogs you select "Journal Title" (or "Periodical Title," which is another name for Journal) instead of "Author, Title, or Subject," and type in "American Psychologist."

Just as in our book search, a screen appears that lists titles close to "American" in alphabetical order. XAC shows that Xavier's library does have this journal, and when we select the line for *American Psychologist* it gives us another screen listing the years and volumes that are available. Here's what it looks like in XAC:

Call Number 150 A512p
Title The American psychologist.
Imprint Arlington, VA, American Psychological Association.
Current Frequency Monthly
Holdings 1-2 of 2

1
Location Periodicals - 2nd Floor
Library Holdings No longer received.
v. 1-32 1946 - 1977 Public Note: microfilm
v. 23-28 1968 - 1973 Public Note: Bound
v. 30 1975 Public Note: Bound
v. 34-44 no. 1979 – 1989 Public Note: Bound
v. 47-55 no. 1992 - 2000 Public Note: Bound
v. 56 no. 1-12 January - December 2001
v. 57 no. 1 January 2002 Public Note: Bound

2
Location Microforms - 2nd Floor
Library Holdings v. 1-32 1946 - January 1977

That all-important call number is on line one, followed by the journal title. "Holdings 1-2 of 2" means that individual volumes are located in two different places. Location 1 is "Periodicals – 2nd Floor." Location 2 is "Microforms – 2nd Floor." Because of budget constraints, universities will not always have every volume of a journal. This is true of *American Psychologist* here. Xavier University has volumes 1-32, which were published between 1946 and 1977, missed Volume 33, and picked up again with volume 34 in 1979. They have up to volume 44 in 1989, but then missed 45 and 46. They added more issues later, but their last volume is number 57, from January 2002. In contrast, Xavier has volumes 1-114 of *The Journal of Abnormal Psychology*, although they stopped taking it after that. For both journals, however, the articles that we're looking for—Fallon and Rozin, and Polivy and Herman—are available.

Not all journal volumes will be in book form in the periodical area, though. Volumes 1-32 of *American Psychologist*, and volumes 1-86 of the *Journal of Abnormal Psychology* are followed by the notation "microfilm." This means the journals for these years are on a type of film that has to be read off on a machine. This is why there is a location called "microforms," although it usually will be close to the periodical area. (A librarian can demonstrate how to work the film machine reader; they're pretty simple.) Other volumes for these two journals, including the ones we want, are listed as "bound." This means they are in book form on the shelves. Just look for the call number from the first line of your search listing. By the way, most libraries have handouts that show the floor plan and where things are located. Ask at the front desk.

Increasingly, libraries are running out of space on their shelves for hard copies of journals and are subscribing to journals online, often called "E-journals." If you tried to access these publications through the internet you'd have to pay a hefty fee—many journals cost $1000 or more for a yearly subscription—but as a faculty member or student at a university you can often use your school I.D. to get free access, either through your computer or through a terminal in the library. In most cases, the university's main library page will have a link to something like "online resources." This generally takes you to a list of "databases." A database is a *collection* of resources such as dictionaries, newspapers and magazines, or...journals. One example is JSTOR, a collection of research articles from academic journals.

A very good database for psychology majors is PsycINFO, which contains references from the majority of important psychological journals. Most big university libraries subscribe to it. Databases are usually listed on library web pages in alphabetical order, so once at the database page scroll down to PsycINFO and click on it. Spend a few minutes exploring the page that comes up. You can search PsycINFO for an author, an article title, a journal, or by subject, and there are a variety of ways to refine and narrow a search. Even if you don't know specific details about an article, PsycINFO is a good place to begin searching for information for papers. It mostly provides abstracts, although some full articles are available. Sometimes abstracts are all you need, but if you want the full article then the PsycINFO entry will provide the information on authors, volumes, and dates that are needed to find the work on a library's shelves or through interlibrary loan.

Online searching of databases is still relatively new and change is constant. Any detailed description of available databases and the process used to access them would be obsolete soon after being written. Generally, though, conducting subject searches on such databases requires entering key terms, like "anorexia" or "eating disorders," and the computer then scans its periodicals and provides a list of articles that consider those topics. This is how PsycINFO works, and in this way one can find sources of information quickly without having to physically page through each periodical. To find out what *your* library has to offer in the way of online searching, check with a librarian. They'll almost certainly have brochures or pamphlets available as guides to the process.

Finding Psychological Scales

For many class assignments, especially for methods classes, or for your own research, you'll need to secure a "scale" or a measure of some psychological variable. For example, if you want to measure people's level of extraversion, you will probably need to find a questionnaire designed to do just that. Doing so may be tricky. Many researchers want to earn a little profit from the scales they develop and may not be willing to make them freely available. Still, a reasonably good scale can usually be found by tracking that scale through publications by researchers who use it.

If you read an article that cites a scale, then try looking up the cited article, which will be listed in the References section. If the people who wrote the "cited" article didn't create the scale, they'll cite yet another article about it. Keep going backwards until you find the names and contact information for the people who developed the scale (Remember that university affiliations are generally listed on page one of an article). Then write or email those researchers to ask about using it.

You could also try a PsycINFO search, typing, for example, "Extraversion and Scale" into the search line. You may have to be creative but with some thought you can usually find a good scale to measure any variable of interest.

Conclusions

What we have been talking about in this chapter is how to locate information on a subject you want to write about. We've looked at finding books and finding articles. Now, think of this, the articles you found, the books you borrowed, all have their own reference sections. If you need more information on a topic, find the references for *those* books and articles, which will, of course, refer to yet other works. Soon, you'll have a large list of potential references and will be culling ones that aren't of use instead of struggling to find a few that are. It's easier to cull than add.

Now, before closing this chapter we want to mention a few related topics on the library that it might help to be familiar with. These are Government Documents, Media Services, and Archives and Special Collections. Each will be dealt with separately in the sections that follow.

Government Documents

One of the biggest publishers in the United States is the U.S. Government, which provides reams of material each year to interested readers. This material includes such things as the report on the September 11 terrorist attacks, the reports of Congressional committees, U.S. budget information, and public service information on all manner of diseases and disorders. Much of this material is disseminated to universities throughout the country where it is held in the libraries under "government documents." Although most of this is available online as well, there is such a huge amount of information that a trained librarian from a university's government document center may be essential to helping find the material you want.

Media Services

The media center supplies "audiovisual" needs for a university community. It will usually have audiotape players and a tape library, DVDs, VCRs, and overhead projectors. There are often separate rooms for viewing films or listening to music. Among the more frequent users of a media center are students learning a foreign language. Students working on papers might find videos on their topics, or audiotapes of interviews with scientists, or a variety of other kinds of information. Our advice is to ask a librarian what is available.

Archives/Special Collections

A library's archives, often called special collections, is a place where valuable and rare materials are kept. These may be signed editions of novels, old books too brittle to be handled, private letters from famous people, or unpublished information that is still in manuscript form.

Most special collections focus on one or more collecting areas. Xavier University's archives, for example, owns African artworks and old manuscripts of various kinds, but generally maintains and collects in four distinct areas: 1) works by, for, or about African Americans, 2) works having to do with the southern U.S. and southern culture, 3) works having to do with U.S. Catholicism, and 4) works having to do with Xavier itself. Every student ought to take a look at their university's archives during their career, whether it's for research purposes or just for fun.

CHAPTER FIVE

WHY OUTLINES AREN'T A WASTE OF TIME

"What is written without effort is read without pleasure."
—Samuel Johnson

Outlines are a waste of time, right? Why spend time figuring out what kind of order things should go in when you could just as easily grab up a textbook for information and start writing. You could follow the order in the text, leave some blank spaces where more information is needed, and have four or five pages done while your roommate is still working on Roman Numeral III.

Sound familiar? This may be the way some of you think today, and it was certainly the way many of us thought and worked back in high school. However, those of us who write every day as part of our jobs know now that we were wrong. The four or five pages you write *after* outlining are going to be much better than the pages written before. That investment translates directly into higher grades. It also helps ensure against the serious mistake of plagiarism. Even following the exact order of a textbook is considered plagiarism, which is why we mentioned it so casually in the previous paragraph.

Spending time outlining and organizing sources is not wasted time. It is the absolutely necessary first step in constructing a reasonably good paper. Whether we realize it or not, we all organize material spontaneously before we start writing. Most of this is done unconsciously, meaning that we're not even aware of it. We just start putting things down, and some kind of coherence develops because our minds are built to associate similar topics together. One thing leads to another.

The more experience you have as a writer, the more likely you are to do a good job at this kind of unconscious organization. The mind becomes trained to know what works because it worked before. New writers do not have experience to draw upon, however, and they are often less likely to use an outline for help. They let the unconscious do all the work, without providing it any structure. Outlines provide that structure, and without one the newer writer is almost certainly going to waste time and effort and still not achieve the best results.

Now, how to go about *doing* an outline is a different story. Some writers like to use the kind of outline they learned in high school (Roman Numeral I, etc.), and that's fine if they feel comfortable with it. Most writers, however, adapt their outlines to the length and complexity of their papers. Experienced writers may need only a title or opening sentence to help them organize a short piece (two or three pages), but they'll certainly need to do more outlining for a longer piece. A beginning writer should probably do an outline for a paper of even 3 pages, though it certainly won't have to be very detailed.

The following paragraphs provide some guidelines and examples to help you develop an outline. These are meant only to offer a place to start. Modify them to fit your personal needs. Also remember, many instructors will be happy to glance at any outline you are developing. Their feedback could be invaluable.

To start, we suggest that the first part of any outline be a working title. This should only be selected after some background reading on the topic of interest, but the title itself will help begin the organizational process. It has to be a good title, though, one that helps define the topic to be covered. The title "Mental Disorders" is too broad. It covers far too much information for a paper of 10 to 15 pages. "Schizophrenia" would be a better title than "Mental Disorders" because it decreases the size of the term paper canvas you are trying to paint. Even better would be such titles as "The Types of Schizophrenia," or "Positive versus Negative Symptoms in Schizophrenia." These are more specific and can provide more guidance in constructing a paper.

Once the working title is in place, jotting down a few quick sentences of information that you already know can help focus your attention on important points. Then head for the library, either for real or from the comfort of your own internet-capable computer, to see how much reference material is available. The best outlines are fluid, growing and changing as fresh information is integrated into them, as the new is linked with what you already know. So keep that rough outline handy, adding possible sources as you find them and revising as you gather facts and make connections between them.

One possible outline for a paper entitled "Schizophrenia" is shown after this paragraph. It was constructed by selecting a topic and jotting down a title and some major points to consider about the topic. Our background reading on the subject was already completed and we had a pretty good idea about where to find the kind of information we might need. Likely sources are listed in our outline in parentheses. (Note: If you're wondering why we switched from anorexia to schizophrenia, well, it just seemed a good time for a change.)

Sample Outline 1

Title = Schizophrenia

1. Give a definition of schizophrenia (Use the textbook).
2. Describe someone with schizophrenia (Use the textbook and library books, and ask psychology professors for examples).
3. List and describe the types of schizophrenia (DSM-IV-TR and textbook).
4. Causes of schizophrenia, talk about theories (Library books and journals).
5. Treatments for the disorder (Library books and journals).
6. Conclusions: Restate basic points. Give my opinions.
7. References section. Include the textbook and DSM.

This is one way to do an outline. It's short and took only a few minutes to construct, but it provides a plan to follow, which is all an outline is supposed to do. For longer works, lengthy term papers or books, a correspondingly longer outline will be needed. Books are broken into chapters, and many books, like this one, have a contents page that is essentially a broad outline of the entire work. In many textbooks this chapter outline is developed in great detail. This helps guide readers through the book, but it was probably first used as a guide by the writer.

Although books naturally divide into chapters, and research reports are born with sections like "Method," "Results," and "Discussion," many people don't realize that standard term papers or most any type of short non-fiction can also benefit from being subdivided. An outline can help here, as well. For example, our paper on schizophrenia could easily have sections dealing with each subtype of the disorder (e.g., paranoid, catatonic). This might look like:

Types of Schizophrenia

Paranoid Schizophrenia
Paranoid schizophrenia is characterized by...
Catatonic Schizophrenia
A second type of schizophrenia is the Catatonic type. It...
Disorganized Schizophrenia
The most severe form of schizophrenic fits into the...

This format uses "headings" (Types of Schizophrenia) and "subheadings" (Paranoid, Catatonic, & Disorganized Schizophrenia) to break the paper into small, manageable sections. And, if you've developed a complete outline then the headings will come directly from it, as we'll see in a moment.

There are no important disadvantages to using headings, and there are many ways in which they can make a piece of writing better. As part of the outline they help organize the paper before the writing starts. In fact, set up the outline in the same computer file where you plan to store your paper—printing out a copy to carry along when you're away gathering data—then use the outline and headings to indicate exactly where the material on a certain discussion point should go. Having separate sections will also help you visualize where more information is needed, or where there may be too much.

Headings are certainly a boon for readers, who can use them to orient themselves easily within a paper. The reader always has a signpost to help point out where he or she is, and to indicate what issue is being discussed. This is one of the most important advantages to headings. After all, the readers are the people you're trying to please.

Before we leave this chapter on better organization through outlining, let's cover one last example. Our first outline was too short to do more than provide some broad guidelines. Let's add a little more depth, a little more detail. We'll need more headings, more references, more everything. The result will be better than our first outline, though it will take longer to construct. That shouldn't bother us, though. The more work we put in on our outline, the less work we'll have to do on the paper and the better the end product will be. Here is a possible example.

Sample Outline 2

Title = Schizophrenia

1. Introduction: Hook the reader with an unusual point or statistic about schizophrenia. Define schizophrenia and provide a little history about the disorder. Use the textbook, library books, history of psychology text, popular books for anecdotes. Or ask psychology professors for examples.

2. Characteristics: Describe the general symptoms and behaviors of schizophrenia but don't go into detail. Discuss here the things that are common to all types. Use the DSM-IV-TR, the textbook, recent findings from journal articles.

3. Types of Schizophrenia. Use a different subsection for each subtype. Discuss details under each section, including symptoms, the frequency of occurrence, the prognosis, and any other items of interest. Report case studies for each type. Use the DSM-IV-TR, library books, textbooks, journals. Use popular books and psychology professors for anecdotes and case studies.

   a. Paranoid - case study, symptoms, prognosis.
   b. Catatonic - case study, symptoms, prognosis.
   c. Disorganized - case study, symptoms, prognosis.

d. Undifferentiated - case study, symptoms, prognosis.
e. Residual - case study, symptoms, prognosis.
4. Causes of schizophrenia. Discuss theories. Touch on possible social or cultural causes (e.g., double bind concept), and on biological theories (e.g., genetics, dopamine hypothesis, brain damage). Use textbooks from history of psychology, from abnormal, physiological, and from personality.
5. Treatments: Discuss in general terms. Tie treatments to the theories discussed under #4 above. Use recent journals as much as possible. Otherwise use textbooks and library books.
6. Conclusions: Restate the major points of the paper. Add conclusions, if any. Close with something upbeat, or at least leave the reader with some comment or anecdote that triggers an emotional response.
7. References section:

Now, we move the complete outline down a page in our computer file and copy just the headings above it to set up a "template" for our paper, which just means creating a pattern for ourselves to follow. This will look like the following:

Schizophrenia

Introduction
Characteristics of Schizophrenia
Types of Schizophrenia
    Paranoid.
    Catatonic.
    Disorganized.
    Undifferentiated.
    Residual.
Causes of Schizophrenia
Treatments for Schizophrenia
Conclusions

If you can put together a detailed outline before starting to write, then the rest of the work will flow more smoothly and easily. The template will act as a guide and you can check back and forth with the outline to see what is needed in each section of the paper. You'll know where you stand at every moment and where to go next, and sections can always be further subdivided if needed. You'll also be able to tell more easily where to discuss each of the sources gathered from the library. (For more specifics on how to use headings please see the APA's *Publication Manual*.)

Outlining doesn't mean the work is done, but it does mean that the initial barrier is broken and the paper is off to a fast start. The next chapter will discuss how to make sure the momentum gained from the outline is not lost as you face the harder work of the first draft. As a last item before we leave this section of the book, however, take a look at the following "Model Outline" form on the next page. Using this model is not a requirement, but it might be helpful to some. At least it provides a place to start. Use any sections you need, discard those you don't, and modify it to fit the specific requirements of your paper. Feel free to make photocopies as needed.

A MODEL OUTLINE

Title of Paper:

Content of Introduction:

Content of Body:

Conclusions:

Sources:

CHAPTER SIX

PREPARING AND WRITING

"The will to win is not worth a nickel unless you have the will to practice"
—Unknown

Part of the writing process is so visceral as to defy any simple "how to" explanation. How do you begin? Where do you begin? And, most importantly, how do you continue through the hard work of building a paper? Though there are no simple answers to these questions, this chapter offers some points to consider and some suggestions on how to proceed. These have been gleaned from your authors' own experiences, and from those of other professional writers. Give them a listen and a try to see if they can work for you, and check out the Bibliography in this *Guidebook* for additional books that can help you learn how to write well. For now, there are three topics we'll be covering in this chapter, 1) time management, 2) the personal aspect of writing professionally, and 3) getting words down and keeping them flowing.

Time Management

We talked about "Time Management" briefly in Chapter 1, but we need to revisit the topic more completely here. We do so because no one can write a word unless they have time, but our lives are busy and finding time is arduous.

Making time is much easier. Think about when you wanted to do some fun activity so badly your hair hurt. Weren't you busy then too? Yet, you made time for the fun. And without adding a physical minute to the day. *Time* is there if you know how to manage the hours already available.

Deciding how to best manage your time is a process of self-discovery that can even be fun. It begins with a realistic look at your daily schedule. Take the worksheet from Appendix A in this book and make as many copies as needed. Also, pick up a calendar on which to mark important dates. On the worksheet, put down those items that must have a place in a day's activities (e.g., sleeping, eating, showering, dressing, classes, chores, transportation, and walking the dog). Be realistic in your estimates. Time yourself. Use a stopwatch if you have one. Next, enter the activities that you engage in every day but which are more flexible, such as studying (about two hours for every hour spent in class), reading, talking to friends, napping, watching television, etc. Here you might include listening to music or playing with the cat.

Repeat this exercise over several days (a full week with weekends included would be best), remembering to add in those tasks such as shopping for food or emptying the trash that aren't done *every* day. Then sit down to see where and how your time is spent. Every hour is probably filled with some activity, but we'll bet that not all of those activities are critical. We'll bet there's plenty of "wasted" time.

Do you really need to watch that *Simpsons* rerun for the third time? How often do you have to check email? Will your best friend actually get mad if you don't "text" her every hour? Cut back on TV, computer games, surfing the 'net, and other non-essential activities, and this will free up time to use for writing (or for other important things.) And for goodness sake, is it absolutely necessary to call someone on the phone every time you have a free moment? Think about it.

Once time has been identified that can be focused toward writing, take out that calendar we suggested and mark off important dates, such as holidays, test days, and paper deadlines. Match the deadlines with your daily schedule and see how much time will be available for each task. During the early part of the semester plan to spend three to four hours a week doing research for each paper that you have. Allow more time toward the end, and set a definite date for when everything will be finished. Make that date at least a couple of days before the assignment is due so that you can fine-tune and proofread at a leisurely pace.

The reason why more work time is needed at the end of the semester is because that's when you really begin to integrate your research and your own creative thoughts about a topic. This is the critical juncture. Think of it as that point in cooking a gourmet meal when all the ingredients have been carefully assembled and laid out delicately on the counter. Now it becomes crucial that you blend, stir, mold, and peel with great precision and refined perception. That's where those extra hours will be helpful.

If you follow a writing schedule faithfully, the results will more than compensate for a few lost phone conversations or for missing that TV show, which, of course, you recorded anyway. (Isn't technology grand?) Time management takes self-discipline and requires self-honesty, but in return it offers a sense of direction and a pleasant feeling of having imposed at least some order on chaos.

Here's a last little hint about managing writing time. Build rewards into your schedule from the beginning. After finishing a section of the paper, go watch a favorite TV show or get an ice cream bar. And after a week of hard work you deserve to see that new movie that just opened. Reward yourself for doing good work and you won't burn out.

The Personal Aspect of Writing Professionally

In addition to time management skills, you need to find ways to get involved emotionally in writing a paper. No matter what the topic is, no matter whether you are writing a term paper, a research report, or for some other kind of project, your own interest and excitement needs to shine through if you are going to produce the best finished product.

For example, a psychology instructor might assign a term paper on Delusional Disorder. A simple clinical description of symptoms, predisposing factors, essential and associated features, age of onset, course, and complications of the disorder can be harvested from the *Diagnostic and Statistical Manual of Mental Disorders IV* (DSM-IV-TR; American Psychiatric Association, 2000). Pretty much anyone can do this. The problem is that such a paper won't have anything uniquely *you* in it. Your personal perspective and personal passion will be missing, and that's what an instructor wants.

Please remember that teachers don't want just to be fed dry facts that they've already eaten and digested. (One teacher described it, memorably, as like swallowing "intellectual vomit.") So, how can you complete an assignment without making this common, and grade-lowering, error? Pay close attention to the human element. Use case studies to enliven the discussion of the topic, and make your report personal. Can you imagine what it is like to suffer from Delusional Disorder? Can you imagine how others would think and act toward you? The data that you're reporting will be the main course of the paper. You'll add the flavoring, the gravy, the side dishes of salad and sweet dessert. These will come from your experiences and imagination. Take the facts, mix them with your own empathy, and put the results down on paper using your own unique language and expressions, not paraphrases of someone else's.

Even when writing a research report or research proposal, where the rules are stricter on what you should and should not say, your personal passion needs to show through. *Why* are you asking the questions that you claim to be asking? What is the importance of this research? Why do you care? Why should anyone? Tell us why, in simple, straightforward language that reveals your personal commitment to the topic.

Teachers don't expect undergraduate students to be perfect in grammar, syntax, and scientific expression. Of course, they want to see your best in those areas, but they also want to experience the world, and issues such as Delusional Disorder, through your eyes. This does not mean that scientific writing is based on opinion or on subjective emotions, but there *is* an important place for individual perception. It is *your* understanding, and *your* writing, that professors want to see.

Getting Words Down and Keeping Them Flowing

Interruptions are the writer's worst enemy. Just when you're ready to work, with your thoughts focused on the topic, the phone rings or someone knocks on the door. Or, even worse, you're already writing and in the flow of the piece when the interruption comes. You lose track of where you were and suddenly your thoughts are eddies where before they were a swiftly moving stream. Take steps before you write to make sure this doesn't happen.

Interruptions come from two places, outside of you, and inside of you. But you can arrange the writing environment to avoid, or at least minimize, both. To avoid external interruptions, set up phones to take messages instead of answering them, and then find a physical location to write where people are unlikely to discover you. Many libraries, for example, have small study rooms called carrels that are available to students. These usually have lights, a desk, a chair, and a place to plug in a laptop. Not much distraction there. (One of your authors routinely uses library carrels for his own work and highly recommends them.)

Now, what about the internal interruptions? I'm talking about those things that writers do to break their own concentrations, such as deciding that they "really need a soda," or they "forgot to get a pen," or they "ought to check their email one more time." These are more difficult to deal with, but a little self-discipline can work wonders.

If you like a sip of water now and then while writing, make sure to have water on your desk *before* starting work. If you like to listen to music, set up the stereo ahead of time and pre-select the songs to listen to. Put a dictionary, thesaurus, the APA manual, and a grammar guide within easy reach so you won't have to "fetch" them. Spread notes and references out in some logical order. (Remember back in Chapter 3 when we suggested organizing your notes by putting them in file folders? Here's where that will pay off.) Shut down email and all other web pages that you aren't actually using for the project. Make sure there's a pen and notepaper handy, and prepare whatever idiosyncratic items that you might want, such as soft lighting or hard candy.

Now you're ready to begin. Writing time has been scheduled and you haven't waited until the last minute to start. You're feeling confident in your ability to complete the project because you've checked with the instructor about anything that was confusing. You've arranged the environment to help rather than hinder you, and you have the physical tools you need (pen and paper, computer, whatever).

The first thing you'll write will be the title. Follow that with the headings developed in your outline. Already the threatening blankness of the page is broken. But where to next? Well, what about a definition of the topic? This will tell the reader up front what *specific* issue you are addressing.

Some writers block on the first sentence because they insist that it be brilliant and creative, that it suck the reader in. Brilliant and creative are great, but you can't wait weeks for inspiration to strike. Get a textbook, find a definition of the topic, and put it down as the first line under the title, properly citing the author of the definition, of course. Starting with a definition is always a safe way to begin, and you can change that first line later when the brilliantly perfect phrase hits you.

Once the definition is down, work with it to make it clear to your readers. Say the paper is on schizophrenia, for example, and the definition contains something like "a psychotic disorder accompanied by hallucinations and delusions." Well, after the definition you should probably explain what "psychotic" means, and what "hallucinations and delusions" are. Then you may want to give an example, so describe a case study. By now, half of the first page is filled and the paper is well underway. What next? History of schizophrenia? Symptoms? You decide.

As the paper gets underway, don't worry too much initially about correcting errors, especially in grammar, spelling, and punctuation. As we suggested earlier in this book, if the sentences sound terrible at first, leave them anyway and go on. If you can't find the perfect word or remember the scientific name for a concept immediately, type in a [blank] or [underline] and keep rolling. Like most kinds of work, writing can develop its own momentum as you practice it. Once the barrier of the empty page is broken the words should start to flow more easily. They may not be great words perfectly organized and polished, but that's to be expected. All first drafts are awkward, but this one you'll reshape into a final masterpiece (or at least into an "A" paper).

Remember that you've set some limits on how much time you'll spend or how much work you'll accomplish in each writing session. Adhere to that. Again, as we've said before, a good paper cannot be finished in one sitting. Pace yourself.

So, how long *should* you work? How much *should* you do? The answers to these questions are different for each writer, and you'll find your own answers through experience. To begin with, we might suggest to try writing for an hour each day, or until you finish one good page. Of course, you may find that you can't manage quite that much, or that you're comfortable doing two hours or two pages, or more. Adjust your schedule as you begin to learn your limits, but remember to *always* put down words in every writing session, even if they don't seem to be any good. Keep making progress and you can reach any goal.

One of your authors has the goal of finishing *at least* one good paragraph every day, no matter the distractions. That's not much, but there are only three to four paragraphs on an average page. One paragraph a day means ten finished pages in a month, and, of course, he often writes more than his minimum.

As you finish each writing session, remember to jot some quick notes at the end as a guide toward the next session's work. Begin each new day of writing by reading over and correcting (if necessary) the previous day's work. This helps you get "warmed up" and will ensure continuity within the paper. Stephen King does this (Underwood & Miller, 1988). Ernest Hemingway did it. Hemingway always stopped writing before he got tired, when he was still interested in finding out what happened next. This helped him leap right into his work the next day (Lynn, 1987).

Finally, adhere to your writing schedule and commitment without exception (short of family tragedy). This is a repetition of what we've already said, but it may be the most important of all the hints and suggestions that we've given. In doing this, you should quickly find that the unusual task of writing has become the ordinary, just another part of your everyday activities, and you will also have begun a remarkable odyssey into your own mind. From there comes the "stuff" that makes any writer's work unique.

CHAPTER SEVEN

GRAMMAR, PUNCTUATION, CLARITY, AND STYLE

"Like everything metaphysical, the harmony between thought and reality is to be found in the grammar of the language."
—Ludwig Wittgenstein

Words are the bricks from which a term paper is built, and there are some rules about how those bricks should be fitted together to construct the "house of ideas" that makes up such a paper. These rules are called syntax and grammar and are usually learned in third or fourth grade. Unfortunately, if you had no need to remember the rules because you were never required to write, or because they were not graded when you did write, you may well have forgotten them. Even worse, at age nine or ten you may have perceived the rules to be a nuisance and simply decided to ignore them rather systematically. This is a problem because college instructors will now assume that you know the rules and how to apply them.

It is far beyond the scope of this small guide to review all the rules that govern English, but there are certain errors that appear so frequently that they need to be addressed in any book concerned with quality writing. These are the errors discussed in this chapter. For more help, contact the English Department at your school. Many such departments have a "writing center," or may be able to provide tutors paid for by university funds. In addition, the Bibliography at the end of this guide lists a number of books that deal with syntax and grammar in a helpful fashion. And remember that a good dictionary can answer many questions about word usage.

COMMON USAGE ERRORS

Subject/Verb Agreement

Among the most frequent grammatical errors encountered by college instructors is the failure of students to make their verbs agree with—or match—their subjects in respect to number and tense. Example: "Term papers is easy to write." "Term papers" is the subject and is obviously plural in number. Plural subjects need plural verbs, but "is" is singular. "Papers" and "is" don't agree in number.

"I would never make such an obvious mistake," you say with appropriate outrage. OK, try this one. Example: "Each one of you are able to write brilliantly." This doesn't sound too bad. But is it correct? No! "Each" is *singular* and needs a singular verb. "Each one of you is able to write brilliantly" is how the sentence should read. Other words like this that require singular verbs are: either, neither, everyone, someone, nobody. These rules mean that writing "Each participant completed their own questionnaire" is wrong. On the other hand, to avoid sexist writing, "Each participant completed *his* own questionnaire" is wrong too. Here, there are two options. One is to keep the singular, but remove the sexism, as in "Each participant completed his or her own questionnaire." Another is to change the sentence to the plural, as in "All participants completed their own questionnaires."

Here's another example of the same problem that probably sounds OK to most of you, but which is still ungrammatical: "As a senior approaches graduation, they are likely to focus on...." The problem is that "senior" is singular, but "they" is plural. The two are mismatched. Yet, you can't correct it by writing "As a senior approaches graduation he is likely to focus on..." because it is sexist to use "he" only. Again, the two ways to fix the problem are to use "he or she," or to change "senior" to "seniors" and keep "they." The plural route is probably the easiest way to solve this difficulty.

The problem of subject/verb agreement is often compounded when "collective" nouns are used. These are nouns like "jury," "committee," "faculty," "assembly" and "team." These words are most often considered as a unit, and thus are singular and need a singular verb. Example: "The team is ready to play." However, one can refer to the *component individuals* of a collective noun and in that situation they become plural and need a plural verb. Example: "The faculty were unsure about the proposed strike." When in doubt, use the singular verb. You'll be right more often than wrong.

Now let's look at a different subject/verb number problem. Example: "Psychotherapy, in conjunction with systematic desensitization, exemplify this treatment modality." Despite the dependent clause ("in conjunction...") that has been added after "Psychotherapy," which makes it sound as if there are two subjects instead of one, there is still a singular subject. The dependent clause is an add-on, not part of the true subject. Removing it will illustrate what we mean. "Psychotherapy exemplify this treatment modality." This doesn't sound right, does it? "Psychotherapy *exemplifies* this treatment modality" is correct. "Psychotherapy" is singular and must have a verb (exemplifies) that agrees.

Though we've been dealing with difficulties in subject/verb "number," subject/verb "tense" is often an even stickier problem. In today's world, "tense" generally refers to some form of nervous strain or worry. In the parlance of syntax, however, tense means the *time* at which some action takes place. Essentially, it means: 1) did you do something in the past, 2) are you doing something now, or 3) will you do something in the future? These are called "past tense," "present tense," and "future tense," respectively. (There are also the "perfect tenses" to consider, but these are seldom seen in term papers or research reports and will not be covered here.) The following are some rules to think about for tense.

Rule 1: Use "past tense" to talk about research that has been completed at the time you are writing. "In 1984, Howard and Smith *developed*...."

Rule 2: Use "present tense" to define terms. "Delusions *are* false beliefs."

Rule 3: Save "future tense" for when you mention planned or potential research that hasn't been done yet. "Future studies *should* investigate...."

Voice

Another common source of confusion that "cries out" to be addressed is the problem of "voice." If the subject of a sentence is performing the act being described, then you are writing in the "active voice." Example: "Rick Holmes admitted himself into the mental facility." Here, Holmes is the one acting. However, if the subject is acted upon, you're writing in the "passive voice." Example: "Rick Holmes was admitted into the mental facility." Holmes is being acted upon by the facility. Though much scientific writing is done in the passive voice, this is not a requirement. In fact, passive writing is generally weak so make every effort to use the active voice instead, which is dynamic, direct, and powerful. One way to do this is by telling the reader *who did something* rather than *what was done.*

Here are some more examples.

Weak: Participants were asked to complete...

Better: Participants completed... OR The experimenter asked participants to complete...

Weak: Participants were given a consent form...

Better: Participants signed a consent form...

Errors in Expression

There are some common mistakes that writers make which don't fit neatly into categories like "Voice" or "Subject/Verb Agreement." We call these "errors in expression" and discuss them in the section that follows.

Although: "Although" is not a transition between sentences by itself; it's different from "however" or "nevertheless"

Wrong: Although, these findings contradicted the researchers' hypotheses...

Better: These findings, however, contradicted the researchers' hypotheses. OR

Better: Although these findings are important, they contradicted the researchers' hypotheses.

Clarifying Comparisons: Note the ambiguity of the following:

"Men will be more likely to show active aggression."

Are men more likely *than women* to show aggression? Or are they more likely to show aggression than they are *friendliness?* The current wording doesn't make it clear.

Consistency within a Series:

Weak: Participants in condition A reported higher levels of depression, anxiety, and frequency of panic attacks.

Better: Participants in condition A reported higher levels of depression and anxiety and higher frequency of panic attacks.

Dangling Modifiers: Good writing avoids imprecise references throughout. In the following example, what is "which" referring to, the phrase, or the screen?

Wrong: Then a phrase appeared on the screen, which they were told to disregard.

Better: Then a phrase, which participants were told to disregard, appeared on the screen.

Getting to the Point: Don't "beat around the bush" when there is a point to make. For example, don't say what a researcher "wanted" or "tried" to do or "were interested in"; instead, say what they *did*.

Weak: The researchers were interested in studying...

Better: The researchers studied...

Also, try to avoid overusing phrases like "seems to" or "it would appear that."

Weak: The researchers would seem to suggest...

Better: The researchers suggest...

If versus Whether:

Weak: The purpose of the proposed study is to determine if...

Better: The purpose of the proposed study is to determine whether...

It: "It" is a dangerous word that you should think carefully about before using. Make sure that what "it" refers to is perfectly clear. Consider the following passages in which "it" is ambiguous, confusing, or just imprecise:

"It has been shown that..."

"When someone suffers from trauma to that extent, it usually changes the..."

"Their view is different in the way they address a range of symptoms, rather than narrowing it down to..."

"They support these findings when it reveals that..."

"When it comes to..."

Male/Female: Better writing uses these words as adjectives ("male participants," "a female experimenter") rather than as nouns ("males responded," "the female administered a survey").

Questions: In formal writing, wording sentences as "questions" or opening sentences with a passive indication of a question is often problematic. Try using simple declarative statements in the active voice instead.

Weak: The question what are the effects of child abuse has not been asked.

Better: Researchers have not resolved the question of child abuse's effects.

Remember: Studies don't investigate something; researchers do. "The study examined…" is wrong.

Use Care with Numbers: The general rule in APA style is to use the numeral when the value is 10 or greater, the word for nine or less. There are a lot of clarifications and exceptions though, so check the *Manual* to be sure.

Use Pronouns Carefully: Note the ambiguity in the following:

"In one study (Wallace & Gromit, 1989), they found…"

Weak: Participants that did…

Better: Participants who did…

Plurals and Other Inconsistencies

One of the main reasons why we English speakers make errors in writing is because our language is inconsistent in how its rules are applied. Look at some of the weird verb usages in English. "I ring the bell, rang the bell, have rung the bell," but "I bring the gift, brought the gift, have brought the gift." The making of plurals is another example. For most plurals you just add "s" (books, ducks, pencils). But sometimes you leave the "s" off (a deer, deer), and sometimes you change the whole form of the word (a goose, geese).

Do you want more examples, some of which are likely to cause confusion for writers in psychology? How about, "The data show that laboratory rats are not as smart as their wild cousins." Why have we used a plural verb (show) when the subject is "data?" Anyone who has taken a class or two in Latin, a language from which English has borrowed many scientific terms, will probably know the answer. Data is the plural form of this word. "Datum" is singular. Words like "criteria," "curricula," and "colloquia" are the same way. So is "phenomena." The singular forms of these words are "criterion," "curriculum," "colloquium," and "phenomenon." (Some other psychological terms with singulars/plurals that are often confused are: "analysis/analyses," "anomaly/anomalies," and "hypothesis/hypotheses.")

Because such words are from an "alien" tongue, but used frequently by scientists and academics, the plural form has begun to sound singular to many people. This is reinforced further by the fictional character, and *single* individual, who is called Data in *Star Trek: The Next Generation*. It still isn't correct.

Another source of confusion is how we in English phrase "general" versus "specific" statements. "Water is wet" (all water in general). "The water is cold" (that specific water). In this case you add the article "the" to make the term specific. But what about, "A dress is a nice thing to have" (dresses in general), and "The dress is at my mom's" (that specific dress). Here you suddenly switch from the article "a" to the article "the" in order to make the same distinction between general and specific. Confusing, isn't it?

The examples we've given here show just some of the inconsistencies that exist in English, most of which are governed by rules that evolved before the language was much like the modern English we know today. Though we often use such terms correctly because of how we were exposed to them in childhood, there is no way short of experience and practice to completely avoid making mistakes with such inconsistent terms. If you have doubts about a word or phrase, looking it up in the dictionary will usually answer your questions on such issues as to how to form a plural or whether the word is a noun or verb. Also, try books like Harry Shaw's *Dictionary of Problem Words and Expressions* (1987), which explains many of the more common word problems that writers face.

Finally, we suggest you start a personal "writing problem" file. As you find answers to grammatical inconsistencies that vex you, perhaps because a teacher calls them to your attention with red ink, put them down in a notebook or computer file started for just that purpose. The very act of writing them down will help you remember them next time, and at worst the answers will be much easier to find when they're needed again.

Periods, Commas, Question Marks, Exclamation Points

Now, if we continue to pursue the original metaphor that we started this chapter with, words as our bricks to build the house of our paper, then we need to look at punctuation as the mortar or cement that holds those bricks together to form a beautiful and coherent architecture. The best papers are "built" primarily out of simple declarative statements that end in periods. The sentence you are reading now is an example. So are the next two. Declarative sentences are like a single thought. A period means the thought is over.

There's nothing wrong in stringing more than one thought together in a sentence, but it becomes confusing if the sentence runs on and on, or if there are no pauses to allow the reader to take a breath. When two or more thoughts are strung together you'll often need to inject an occasional "space to breathe," a kind of writer's window within the bricked structure. This requires a comma, a place to pause before moving to the next thought. Each of the sentences in the paragraph you've just read used commas in this way, including the one you're reading now.

"Elementary," you say? Periods and commas are easy! Well, so are question marks and exclamation points. Question marks appear after direct questions (Did you write today?). Exclamation points are used to add emotional emphasis (Of course, I wrote!). Question marks show up in many places, both in fiction and non-fiction. Exclamation points appear primarily in fiction, usually in dialogue, but are not commonly used in term papers or research reports. Some punctuation marks that you *might* well see in a term paper or research report are semicolons, colons, quotation marks—and those nasty dashes and ellipses? However, there are simple rules for using these, too.

Semicolons

Semicolons join complete, independent clauses when connecting words such as "and" or "but" are not used. For example: "As a patient, Steve Reasoner took accurate notes on the actions of the other patients; he also watched and recorded the behaviors of the staff members." If the semicolon was exchanged for a period and the "he" was capitalized there would be two separate sentences, each of which acts as an independent clause in the larger sentence. When using a semicolon, though, always check to make sure that there are two *complete* sentences being connected. Otherwise you'll end up with a dangling phrase like: "Reasoner took notes on the other patients; on staff members too."

Why use semicolons then? Why not just separate the sentences? The reason is that semicolons emphasize or contrast the connection between two thoughts a little more strongly than if they were separated by a period. And sometimes a writer wants to call just that kind of attention to thoughts.

Colons

Despite the similarity in names, colons do very different kinds of work than semicolons and the two shouldn't be confused. Colons are versatile enough to be used in business letters (Dear Mr. Hawk:), in business memos (TO: & FROM:), in time measurement (it's 12:20), in APA style references where they separate place and publisher (New York: Bantam Books), and in separating titles from subtitles (*Multiple Needs Assessment: A Community Mental Health Concept*). As the following examples show, they are also used to introduce a list, just prior to a quote, and to call attention to the phrase that follows the colon.

Introducing a List. "There are both negative and positive psychosocial stressors: college graduation, marriage, birth of the first child, spousal abuse, divorce, job promotion, etc."

Prior to a Quote. "The teacher did tell us one interesting thing: 'School is out on Thursday.'" Note, though, that the colon should be used only after a complete sentence (independent clause) that introduces the quote. If the sentence isn't complete then a comma should be used instead. "She told him to, 'Go play in the street.'"

Calling Attention to a Phrase. "There are two kinds of people in this world: those who love cats and those who don't."

Quotation Marks

Quotation marks are generally used for three purposes in writing, to set off words that are used in some special way, to identify material that is taken verbatim from someone else's written words, or to identify the direct speech of individual people. Here are some examples.

Word Used in a Special Sense. "Chaos" is a scientific theory.

Words Taken Verbatim From Another Person's Written Work. One of the more famous opening lines in literature comes from Ernest Hemingway's (1952) *The Old Man and the Sea*: "He was an old man who fished alone in a skiff in the Gulf Stream and he had gone eighty-four days now without taking a fish."

Direct Report of a Person's Spoken Words. The client said, "My bones are drying up."

There are several rules for using quotation marks that people often fail to follow. First, periods and commas should appear *inside* quotation marks, as seen in the previous two examples. Second, semicolons and colons always appear *outside* quotation marks. Third, if quoting more than 39 words from a source don't use quotation marks at all but, instead, indent the quote on both sides and put the page number in parentheses at the end. (See the ellipsis section in this chapter for an example.) Fourth, when one quote appears inside another one put single (') quotation marks around the inside quote. For example: The client said, "I hate it when my wife tells me to, 'Get a life.'"

Dashes and Hyphens

The dash is one of the least used but most frequently confused types of punctuation. In manuscript form it is typically written as two side by side hyphens (--), although many word processors will convert these to a single long dash (—). The long dash is sometimes called an "em" dash, and the shorter one the "en" dash. Here we will refer to the long one as the "dash," and the short one as a "hyphen."

"Dashes" often come in pairs, and some style manuals, including APA style, insist that they be connected to the words near them. For example: "We lost the game—by a huge margin—to Denver." Other style manuals, more commonly in the United Kingdom, want spaces around the dash, as in, "We lost the game — by a huge margin — to Denver." Use APA style for your dashes.

Though the dash should be used sparingly, it can serve an important function, usually to highlight or emphasize a piece of information. Example 1: "The client's family—three brothers and four sisters—is very close knit." Example 2: "Daniel tried very hard to win his mother's approval—and failed." A dash can also be used to indicate an "aside," which is when an author injects personal comments or views into writing that is generally intended to be objective. Example: "The survey found that many people who were against abortion also supported the death penalty—a view that I find personally disturbing."

The hyphen is very different from the dash. It's used to connect two words into one word (red-hot, ice-cold) in a way that emphasizes the relationship between them. It used to be common to hyphenate such terms as African American or French Canadian, but this practice is generally frowned upon today and APA style considers the hyphens unacceptable in such cases.

The Ellipsis

An ellipsis is an omission of words. It's indicated by either three periods (...) or four periods, depending on whether it comes in the middle or at the end of a sentence.

It is usually seen in formal papers when words are left out of a direct quote. Let's say, for example, that you want to quote some but not all of the following passage from *On Writing Well* (Zinsser, 1990):

> Writing is hard work. A clear sentence is no accident. Very few sentences come out right the first time, or even the third time.   Remember this as a consolation in moments of despair. If you find that writing is hard, it's because it *is* hard. It's one of the hardest things that people do. (p. 13)

Using the ellipsis, you could produce something like the following. "Writing is...one of the hardest things that people do." Or you might try, "Writing is hard work. A clear sentence is no accident. Very few sentences come out right the first time...." An ellipsis indicates where words have been left out of the quoted section. (Note the three periods used when words are left out in mid-sentence, and the four periods when the ellipsis comes at the end.)

Italicizing for Emphasis

To emphasis a specific word within a sentence, italicize it. For example: "Romeo felt that he could *never* love anyone other than Juliet." Though this is a perfectly good reason to use italicizing and appears throughout this *Guidebook*, it should be used sparingly or it will lose its effectiveness. Italics are also used, of course, to indicate the titles of books (as in the prior sentence), periodicals, and movies.

In closing our discussion of grammar and punctuation, the best thing for avoiding mistakes is to say what you mean in simple, clear sentences. Use the active voice, and make most of the punctuation be periods and commas. If you're not sure about something, get help. Look it up in a dictionary or textbook, or ask a teacher or friend who knows.

STYLE

The issue of "style" is very different from the problems of grammar and punctuation, but it is important to consider in any discussion of good writing. The word itself may make you think of fancier terms like panache or verve, meaning flamboyant or distinctive expression, or it may conjure up images of fashion models stalking down runways in New York and Paris. You're on the right track, but style is also a personal way of expressing yourself or being yourself in any activity you engage in.

For those of you who are female, think of the "statement" you make when you blend certain colors in a novel way or use a silk scarf to accent an otherwise drab jacket or neckline. If you are male, remember when you started a trend by turning up a collar or a shirt-sleeve cuff that was traditionally turned down. This is style in dress.

Style in writing comes when authors put their own creative stamp on the words and phrases they're using. They may combine words in unique ways, or turn common phrases backward to express new thoughts. They may use mostly short sentences, or mostly long ones. They may like to punctuate with dashes. Style expresses an author's personal way of "acting on" words.

To get a feel for how different two writers' styles can be, read a few pages of something by Ernest Hemingway (1899-1961) and then do the same thing for William Faulkner (1897-1962). These two men lived at virtually the same time in history, but isn't the contrast between their styles glaring? Hemingway's prose is simple, economical, and precise. Faulkner's is complex and convoluted. They're different, but neither can clearly be considered better than the other. Both men won the Nobel Prize within a half dozen years of each other.

Style will begin to develop in your writing as soon as you let your personal thoughts and expressions come through on the page, rather than just paraphrasing someone else's words. It *won't* appear overnight. A writing style is refined and distilled with practice. It doesn't consist of cultivated mannerisms. New writers, more often in fiction than in non-fiction, sometimes try to "craft" a style for themselves by deciding ahead of time that they are going to write primarily in sentence fragments, or use only the present tense. Such styles are "artificial," and they often read that way on the page. Let your own style grow and change, and remember that it will vary naturally depending on the kind of writing you are doing. There's nothing wrong with that. Style should be flexible. After all, would you send a formal memo to a picky boss that was worded the same way as a chatty letter to a friend?

Dear Sir:

I wish to inform you that I will not be able to meet with you on April 28, as I will be out of town for a conference.

Hey Bob,

Just wanted to let you know that I won't be able to get together with you in April. Gotta head out of town that week for some stupid conference.

As we've mentioned before, the style of this *Guidebook* is midway between formal and friendly. We've allowed ourselves to break some of the rules of strictly formal writing to make the text seem less daunting, but you should not do this in *your* scholarly papers until first learning the rules extremely well. Like memos to your boss, formal pieces of writing have their own stylistic demands. They should obey all the rules of proper grammar. They should have complete sentences, no contractions (it's, can't), and generally avoid using the first (I) and second (you) person. They should avoid slang and colloquialisms, which are terms or phrases specific to one geographic region that wouldn't be understood in another. For example, in New Orleans some people speak of "making groceries" rather than buying groceries. "Making groceries" shouldn't be used in formal writing because it is likely to confuse readers outside a narrow geographic area.

Although term papers and research reports involve strictly formal writing, they need not adhere completely to a stilted, pedagogical style that mimics all those boring articles you hated to read. Inject some excitement! Use active phrasing. Add anecdotes. Tell a story. Create a scholarly style that combines fascinating information and your own unique perspective with correct grammar and precise wording. This will keep the reader hooked till the end of the paper and will leave them with a sense of having read something worthwhile.

Because style is so personal, new writers sometimes ask how they can tell what is good style from what is bad. There probably isn't any final word on good and bad style, but here are some general guidelines. Most professional writers say that good style avoids trite and worn-out phrases like "drown one's sorrows" or "rub the wrong way." Good style avoids wordiness. Using a phrase like "it is interesting to note that" is a complete waste of time and space. Just start with whatever word comes after "that." Truly effective writing is concise and economical.

In *The Elements of Style* (1979), one of the best books ever written about writing, Strunk and White urge authors to write simply. They tell us that good style, especially in non-fiction writing (though the same ideas apply generally to fiction as well), doesn't try to be flamboyant. It doesn't try to impress the reader. It uses the right words in the right places. This might mean using a big word like "phenomenology," if that's the precise term you want, but it doesn't *require* big words. It doesn't require fancy, convoluted phrases. Although "Due to the fact that" may sound good to the writer, "Because" reads more easily. Although it may sound intelligent to write, "It was discovered in a study by Bourgeois and Thibodeaux (1978) that...," "Bourgeois and Thibodeaux (1978) found..." makes for a much more streamlined paper. Simplifying your sentence structure, avoiding the passive voice, and eliminating unneeded elements will dramatically improve the readability level of your work.

Here are some more examples and suggestions:

Change "...have the tendency..." to "...tend..."

Change "A study by Rogers found..." to "Rogers found..."

Change "There were 100 participants who took part..." to "One hundred participants took part..."

Change "There has been a lot of research done that investigated..." to "Many studies have investigated..."

Striving to use words with clarity and simplicity doesn't mean that your writing can't be lyrical and beautiful, or even poetic. The point is that the writing should serve the needs of the reader rather than the ego of the writer. Let your own style develop out of your need to say important things to those readers as clearly and interestingly as possible.

CHAPTER EIGHT

PROBLEM WORDS AND TERMS

"...using words and expressions effectively depends not on 'correctness' alone but on having something of value to communicate and doing so with ease and assurance."
—Harry Shaw

The English language is lyrical, diverse, flexible, and often beautiful. At times it's also irritatingly complex and outright mystifying—a challenge to all would-be writers who attempt to use it as their medium. Unfortunately, this chapter probably won't completely eliminate your confusion. It *will* discuss some commonly misused words and terms that, because of their difficult spellings and meanings, particularly plague writers in psychology and other sciences. The words are arranged alphabetically below:

Affect/Effect: Confusion between affect and effect is so frequent that they were the first problem words to occur to your authors in writing this chapter. Even careful writers sometimes misuse them. Their pronunciations and spellings are only slightly different, but the meanings are extremely dissimilar. (Such words are called homonyms.) Affect is almost always a verb—except in psychology where it is sometimes a noun. Effect can be a noun or verb with equal ease. Outside of its special use in psychology, affect means "to influence" or "cause a response." For example, "The development of birth control pills *affected* sexual practices in the United States." Affect also means "to pretend" or "to assume," as follows: "He *affected* the attitudes of a hip hop star."

In psychology, affect is also a noun that refers to behaviors such as facial expressions, pitch and volume of voice, and body and hand movements. We use these to make inferences about how another person feels, as in "The client's *affect* did not change when told of his mother's death." Effect, when used as a noun, means "result." For example, "The *effect* of a drug depends on the dosage." Used as a verb, effect means "to cause," as in "The new president will *effect* sweeping changes in personnel and departments."

Then—just to reemphasize our earlier point about the mystifying nature of English—if effect is used in its plural form it can mean "property" or "goods." Here it serves as a noun: "I have willed my *effects* to the family dog."

Among/Between: *Among* is usually used when discussing relationships that involve more than two people or things, such as "The four sisters did not get along *among* themselves." *Between* is used when relationships involve only two things, as in "Just *between* you and me, she doesn't get along with her sisters." The "tween" part of between actually means "two."

Compare/Contrast: Many teachers are fond of telling their classes to compare and contrast various theories. The words do have similar meanings, but there are enough differences to cause confusion. When comparing two things you tend to focus on how they are similar. When contrasting them you focus on how they are different. We might *compare* chimps to gorillas by talking about their physical characteristics and genetic similarities. Many people would prefer, however, to look at the *contrast* between chimps and ourselves, focusing on the differences in culture, technology, and intelligence.

Compose/Comprise: Many people confuse these words. In psychological writing, they may come up, for example, when you describe your sample. It is incorrect to say that "the sample will be comprised of 100 undergraduates." Instead, say that the sample "will be composed of 100 undergraduates" or that it "will comprise 100 undergraduates." These 100 undergraduates will "compose" the sample; the sample will "comprise" them.

Confidant/Confident/Confidential: If you are planning on clinical psychology as a career, then you will undoubtedly become a *confidant* for clients, and you should feel *confident* that your training has prepared you for that role. You should also keep the secrets that a client reveals *confidential*. A confidant "establishes rapport and earns the trust of a client." He becomes someone that the client can feel comfortable "confiding" in. (We use "he" here because a female confidant is called a confidante.) Confusion can occur because when you confide (trust) in people you expect them to keep the information confidential, meaning "they won't tell anyone else." The most commonly heard of these terms, of course, is confident. In this *Guidebook* we've talked about the need to be confident in your ability to express yourself in writing. This means being "assured" of your skills, or "certain" of success.

Council/Counsel: *Counsel* is the term more commonly heard among psychologists. It can be a noun that means "advice," or a verb that means "to advise." Examples would be: "Thanks for your *counsel*; I'm getting along better with my mom now," or "Can you *counsel* me on what courses to take to graduate?" *Council* refers to a group of people who are charged with a certain task, as in: "The student *council* will handle the decorations for the prom."

Confusion also occurs between *councilor* and *counselor*. A councilor is simply a member of a council. A counselor is someone who "counsels," meaning that they give advice or help. Clinical psychologists are sometimes referred to as counselors, though that term is more commonly attached to lawyers.

Covert/Overt: These words are opposites. One way to remember them is to think of covert with a "c" as being under the "<u>c</u>overs," and overt with an "o" as being out in the "<u>o</u>pen." Covert means "hidden" or "concealed." It's something "secret." "It was a *covert* operation; no one but the president and her first husband knew about it." Overt means "open to view." It's made "public" rather than kept secret. "Anti-minority prejudice used to be more *overt* in this country."

Deductive/Inductive: These terms refer to types of logical reasoning. Deductive reasoning moves from the general to the specific, while inductive moves from the specific to the general. For example, I observe twelve different mammals and see that in each case the mammal reproduces by bearing live young. From these specific examples I reason that all (or most) mammals bear live young. This is *inductive* reasoning. Now, knowing that mammals bear live young, if someone tells me that a kangaroo is a mammal then I'll reason that it also bears live young. This would be *deductive* reasoning, going from a general rule to a specific example. Inductive reasoning is how scientific theories are generally built, while deductive reasoning is how they are applied to new situations.

Delusion/Hallucination/Illusion: The terms delusion and illusion may sound alike but there is a clear distinction. A *delusion* is a false belief about external reality that is held so tenaciously that the person won't accept any proof of the belief being wrong. Bizarre delusions are common symptoms of psychoses—severe mental disorders that involve a person losing touch with reality. A person who believes himself to be an extraterrestrial alien from Mars would be characterized as having a delusion.

An *illusion* is when someone misinterprets a real external stimulus. An example would be when the real sound of rustling leaves makes you think that someone has called your name. Illusions are very common and seldom reflect any sign of a mental disorder. They're simply a mistake by our perceptual systems. Illusions are actually used by scientists to help them study the brain; they illustrate how the brain is designed to pay attention to certain stimuli (the sound of voices, for example).

In contrast to delusion and illusion, an *hallucination* is a false sensory experience. This usually means hearing or seeing something that is not real and that is not triggered by any observable stimulus in the environment. For example, a man who "hears" the voice of his dead mother would be experiencing an hallucination. Although it is possible for *anyone* to have an hallucination, this, too, is a common symptom of psychoses. A difference is that when non-psychotic people have hallucinations they usually find them frightening or confusing while a psychotic may accept the hallucination as real without questioning it.

Discreet/Discrete: This is another pair of easily confused homonyms. They are pronounced exactly alike, and though they have different meanings they are both widely used in the field of psychology. Discrete means "separate," "apart," "detached," or "distinct." Example: "Psychology, political science, and sociology are *discrete* disciplines within the social sciences." Another example might be, "The subjects were tested at *discrete* intervals during the day."

In contrast, you probably encountered the word "discreet" before ever hearing of psychology. It's part of the vocabulary that parents use in child-rearing. "Be *discreet* when talking about politics to Grandpa." Being discreet means to be "prudent," "careful," "somewhat circumspect"—to use a "walk on eggshells" or "velvet gloves" approach. Clinical psychologists have to be "discreet" because people often share secrets with them that would be devastating if made public. Research psychologists also have to be discreet because they must protect the identity of research participants.

Disinterested/Uninterested: If you were on trial for a crime that you didn't commit, would you rather have a judge who was *disinterested* in your case, or *uninterested* in your case? Maybe it will help to know that disinterested means "impartial" or "unbiased," while uninterested means "not caring." Choose the disinterested judge every time.

e.g./et al./etc./i.e.: These common abbreviations of some Latin terms are often confused, but they can be useful in scholarly papers. E.g. comes from *exempli gratia*, which means "for example." Et al. is from *et alia*, meaning "and others," and etc. comes from *et cetera*. It means "and other things of the same type." I.e. derives from *id est*, "that is." Here are some examples of how to use these terms:

1. Many brain areas (e.g., the amygdala) are involved in the expression of emotion.

2. No significant results were found (Burke et al., 1999).

3. The patient had marbles, safety pins, paper clips, erasers, etc., in every pocket.

4. The patient's emotional hemisphere (i.e., the right hemisphere) was damaged by a stroke.

In APA style, these abbreviations are almost always used inside parentheses or in tables; the entire phrases for e.g. and i.e. ("for example" or "that is") are usually written out in the text itself. One exception to this is with et al. when it's used for citations in text. Remember that when there are more than two authors for a piece you write out all the names the first time and then subsequently cite only the first author's name accompanied by et al. For example, if Gruber, Arney, and Hall wrote an article that you cited, you would list all three authors on first appearance but would later cite them as either: "Gruber et al. (2006) found…," or as "It was found that… (Gruber et al., 2006)." *Never* abbreviate in the reference list, of course. All names are written out there.

Elicit/Illicit: Another pair of words that sound alike and yet have no relationship in what they mean are elicit and illicit. Both are used frequently in psychology, especially in referring to *illicit* (meaning "illegal") drugs, or to *eliciting* a response from a patient, meaning to "draw forth," "bring out," or "trigger" a response.

Exhausted/Exhaustive: Perhaps one day an instructor will assign you to do an *exhaustive* search of the literature regarding a specific topic such as Rational Emotive Therapy. Even though it's quite probable that you will be *exhausted* when you conclude this marathon search, the two words mean something very different. Exhaustive means "comprehensive" or "thorough." You look at all possibilities. *Exhausted* means "extreme fatigue, the feeling of having used up all of one's energy"—an emotional state that is not foreign to most college students.

Explicit/Implicit: Making something *explicit* means making it "clear" or "specific." An *explicit* set of rules is either written down or is clearly stated and understood by everyone. It is out in the open where nothing is hidden. "Thou shalt not kill," is an example of an *explicit* rule. When something is *implicit*, this means it is "understood" (or supposed to be understood) by everyone without being written down. For example, most groups of humans have rules that everyone understands but no one says. The un-written or informal dress code at a business is a good ex-ample. Everyone dresses at about the same level of for-mality, even though the form of dress is not specified in the employee handbook. Such rules are *implicit*.

Extant/Extent: When doing a literature review for a paper, we suggest you try to cover as much of the *extant* literature as possible. This will increase the *extent* of your knowledge about psychology. Extent means "scope" or "range." Extant is totally unrelated. It means "still in exis-tence," "not lost," "not destroyed." To explore the extant literature on a subject means to look at all the literature available on that subject. Extant is also used sometimes in biology. "Dinosaurs no longer exist on Earth, while their probable descendents—birds—remain *extant*."

Factitious/Fictitious: In the DSM-IV-TR (American Psychiatric Association, 2000), there is a category of men-tal disorders called "Factitious Disorders," which includes disorders that are "characterized by physical or psycho-logical symptoms that are intentionally produced or feigned" (p. 513). This term should not be confused with fictitious. *Fictitious* means "not real," "not true," or a "product of one's imagination." *Factitious* means "artificial," "contrived," or "not spontaneous." Just remember that people can make money off of one (*fictitious*), and end up in a mental hospital for the other (*factitious*.)

Former/Latter: These terms are supposed to be used only when speaking of *two* items, not three or more. *Former* refers to the first of the two items while *latter* refers to the second of the two. When talking about apples and oranges, apples are the *former* and oranges are the *latter*. On the other hand, if there are more than two items or categories being compared, then *former* and *latter* are wrong. In such cases, *first* and *last* are appropriate.

Imply/Infer: One way to remember the difference between these two words is to imagine yourself as a speaker saying: "I imply, you infer." The difference lies in who (or what) is *acting*, and who is interpreting the actions. *Imply* means to "suggest" or "hint" without stating clearly. Only the person or thing that is *acting* can imply. *Infer* means to "draw conclusions from information provided." Only the person who is not acting, who is watching, can infer. For example, a politician might *imply* in her speech that her opponent is a liberal with a capital "L." You might *infer* from her attack on her opponent that she is a conservative. A common mistake student writers make is to say something like: "The data infer...." It should be *imply*, since the data is the actor in this case. The *reader* infers from the data.

Negative/Positive: Although these are common words, they each have special roles in psychology that lead students to confuse their meanings. In everyday usage, positive means "good" and negative means "bad." But in such terms as "negative and positive reinforcement," or "negative and positive correlation," if you think of good and bad you will make an error.

Negative reinforcement occurs when an action causes something unpleasant to be removed from a situation. An example would be when someone takes medicine that gets rid of a headache. The negative here means that something unwanted (the headache) was "removed" or "subtracted" after an action (taking medicine). *Positive* reinforcement occurs when an action brings about a reward. For example, you return a lost wallet and the person who owns the wallet gives you twenty dollars. From your point of view as the person who is acting, something has been "added," and it goes right into your pocket.

Negative *correlations* are those in which two variables change in opposite directions. For example, as people age in years their number of brain cells decreases. In positive correlations, both variables change in the same direction. For most people, as their age in years increases so does their weight in pounds.

Neurotic/Psychotic: Though these terms have different and specific meanings, in common usage they are often treated as if they are the same. A major reason why they've lost their special meanings for many people is because of the corrupting influence of TV and movies, where they are often used incorrectly. (Another psychological term that has suffered the same fate is psychopath.) Because of this corruption, psychologists don't use these terms as frequently as they once did. When they are used formally, though, they do have precise meanings.

A psychotic suffers from a psychosis (plural "psychoses"), a severe mental disorder that is accompanied by a break with reality. The psychotic has hallucinations and delusions, and believes these experiences and thoughts to be real. Psychotic disorders are rare but almost always require hospitalization. Schizophrenia is an example. Psychotic disorders are often associated with biological causes such as genetic abnormalities or chemical imbalances.

In contrast, the neurotic suffers from a neurosis (plural "neuroses"), which does not involve a break with reality. The neurotic may engage in odd behaviors, such as showing a phobic fear to harmless objects, but the person knows that their behaviors and fears are irrational. Neurotic disorders are less likely than psychoses to be associated with biological causes, and usually do not require hospitalization.

Prefixes: A number of *prefixes* that are commonly attached to psychological terms can be confusing. Among these are: extra-/intro-, hyper-/hypo-, inter-/intra-.

Extra-, commonly seen in "extraverted," means "directed outward" or "outside." *Intro-*, seen in "introverted," means "directed inward" or "inside." Thus, "introspection" is when a person looks "inside" themselves.

Hyper- means "too much;" *hypo-* means "too little." For example, a person with "hyperphagia" eats excessively. A child who is "hyperactive" is *too* active. On the other hand, a person with "hypoglycemia" has abnormally *low* levels of blood sugar.

Finally, i*nter-* means "between" while *intra-* means "within." An "interpersonal" relationship occurs between at least *two* people, just as "international" is something that occurs between or among different nations. "Intrapersonal" refers to something within a single person, just as "intravenous" relates to an injection that goes into the vein of a single individual.

Principal/Principle: Again, here are words that sound just alike but have very different meanings. It might help to remember that a princip"a"l, with an "a," is usually a hum"a"n, also with an "a." The head of your high school was a *principal*, which means "chief" or "director." Or perhaps your "pal" from high school was the prince"pal" player on your neighborhood basketball team. This means he or she was the "primary" or "leading" player. A principle, on the other hand, is a "basic truth," or "law." "Matter is neither created nor destroyed" is a *principle* of physics. "Stealing is wrong" might be someone's personal principle.

Psychiatrist/Psychologist: Though frequently misapplied, these terms relate to two different types of scientifically trained individuals. *Psychiatrists* are always M.D.s (doctor of medicine). They can prescribe drugs. Psychologists are trained as Ph.D.s (doctor of philosophy). In recent years, some states (New Mexico and Louisiana) have granted prescription rights to clinical psychologists who have obtained additional training, but most Ph.D.s do not prescribe drugs and have no interest in doing so.

The main difference between the two lies in their training. A medical degree is essentially a practitioner's degree. The M.D. learns how to apply knowledge but is rarely involved in laboratory research where knowledge is generated. A Ph.D. is an academic degree. The Doctor of Philosophy is trained in how to conduct research that produces *new* knowledge. In addition, psychiatrists are usually educated in one specific area of psychotherapy (often neuropsychology) while a psychologist receives broader training in the history, theory, and research methods of psychology. Psychologists will then specialize in a subject area such as Social or Forensic. Either of these two types of professionals can be referred to as "doctor."

The Ph.D. is actually the older of the two degrees, though many people don't realize it. Just in the past few decades, a new degree has been created called a Psy.D. (Doctor of Psychology). Like the M.D., this is also a practitioner's degree, more involved with applying rather than generating knowledge. Psy.D.s are exposed to a broad range of clinical and counseling techniques but are not as deeply trained in research methods as Ph.D.s.

Qualitative/Quantitative: Qualitative relates to the "quality" of something, and quantitative to the "quantity" or "amount." Both are terms frequently heard in psychology, where researchers refer to *qualitative* variables like color and to *quantitative* variables like height, weight, and volume. Most scientists prefer quantitative data to qualitative because meaningful numbers can be assigned to the former. But it's not always easy to do this for psychological concepts. How would numbers be meaningfully attached to something like personality, for example? With quantitative variables, the numbers mean things. Twelve inches is longer than four inches. Ten pounds is twice as heavy as five pounds. Color is a good example of how this doesn't work for qualitative concepts. Is red more than blue? Is green twice as much as yellow?

Stimulant/Stimulus: A *stimulant* causes a temporary increase in an organism's activity levels. The person (or animal) moves around more, or thinks faster. There are *stimulant* drugs, such as nicotine, caffeine, and amphetamine. And there are other *stimulants*, such as the splash of cold water on your face in the morning, or the sounds of certain energetic strains of music. A *stimulus* (plural "stimuli") is anything that "triggers" or "produces" a response. A sudden loud sound will make you jump. The sound is a *stimulus*. A puff of air blown into your eye will make you blink. The puff of air is the *stimulus*. *Stimulus* is the more common term in psychology, and it has specific uses that make it important to know.

Subconscious/Unconscious: Both of these terms are used specifically in psychology, and they have precise meanings. *Subconscious* refers to thoughts or memories that we are not thinking of right now, but which we could easily call to awareness if we wanted. For example, you probably aren't thinking of the mascot of your high school football team, until it's mentioned. It comes to mind easily, though.

Unconscious is different. It has two common meanings, one general and the other specific to psychology. The general meaning of unconscious is being "without awareness," like being "knocked out" by a blow to the head. Someone who "passes out" from drinking will also be labeled unconscious in this sense. In psychology, the term unconscious is also used specifically to represent memories, feelings, and urges that we cannot become aware of easily, but which still can affect our behavior. This meaning comes from Freudian theory, though the term itself does not. For example, a child who was sexually abused may not consciously recall the abuse when they are an adult, but they still may have trouble being intimate in a relationship. The problems come from their *unconscious* memories of the abuse, which still influence their behavior (Gay, 1988).

That/Which: Although many people use these two words interchangeably, they actually serve different purposes and a writer should consider which one is appropriate for a given sentence. *That* allows the writer to specify a particular item out of a group of possibilities. For example: "Schizophrenia is a disorder *that* many people erroneously think means multiple personalities." *Which*, on the other hand, allows the writer to describe the item to which it refers. For example: "The studies, *which* all drew the same conclusion, employed a variety of procedures." As a rule of thumb, if the phrase containing the term needs to be set off by commas, then *which* is probably the better choice.

Timber/Timbre: These words look and sound alike, but only one of them is generally seen in psychology. This is *timbre*, which refers to the complexity of a sound, as when several tones and intensities are combined together. *Timber* is wood.

Conclusions

Though there are many other words and combinations of words that give writers problems, the above are some that particularly trouble those of us in psychology and similar disciplines. See the Bibliography in this *Guidebook* for a list of resources that can help with all kinds of writing questions. Two particularly good sources for help, which we've already mentioned but which deserve another hearing, are *The Elements of Style* by Strunk and White (1979), and *Dictionary of Problem Words and Expressions* by Harry Shaw (1987). Their advice, and ours, is to choose your words carefully and use them precisely. The result will be communication that is clear and effective.

CHAPTER NINE

REWRITE, REWRITE, REWRITE—AND AFTER

You write with ease to show your breeding,
But easy writing's curst hard reading.
> —Richard Brinsley Sheridan

Good writing always means rewriting. There's no way around it. Only the incredibly lucky few—and none of us are among them—can sit down and churn out perfect copy the first time. Most of those who say they can are lying. It just doesn't work that way, for almost anyone, and it doesn't matter whether you are writing term papers, textbooks, or terror novels. The first draft of a writing project is really thinking, not writing. You are thinking on paper, or on a screen, and thoughts just don't come out of people's heads perfectly organized. If there is one absolute rule for improving your writing, it is to do multiple drafts of everything.

Something that happened to one of your authors in graduate school may serve to illustrate the reason why multiple drafts are a good idea. It occurred when your author said to a female friend of his that she must hate getting up in the morning and having to take time to put on makeup. It seemed a bit unfair to him, since most men just comb their hair, and, maybe on a good day, put on some deodorant before leaving the house.

The woman's response was enlightening, however, not really about the fairness or unfairness of putting on makeup, but about the reasons why a writer should always do more than one draft of a piece of work. She said that she *liked* to put on makeup. She'd get up in the morning, look in the mirror, and go, "Yuck." Then she'd fix her hair, put on a little of this and a dab of that, follow it all with a touch of lipstick, and by the time she was done she could look in the same mirror and say, "OK, not so bad."

This is actually a pretty good analogy for writing. First drafts of a term paper, or of any piece of writing, are your early morning face. They have at least a little bit of that "yuck" quality. But then the polishing starts. You get rid of a few excess words, what writers call "fat." You break that long sentence into two shorter ones that are more clear and to the point. You try to figure out what in the world you were thinking when you wrote that first paragraph. By the time the polishing is finished you should have a product that is more likely to evoke "OK, not so bad" than it is to call up "yuck."

How many drafts of a paper should one do? The only answer is to keep rewriting until the work is finished. When asked point-blank, professional writers usually say something like "three." But any number is inaccurate if accepted as a *rule*. The number of drafts depends on the writer and on the piece being written. It probably even depends on what section of the paper is being considered. For example, most writers reword openings and endings much more than they do middles. This is because they know, as you should know, that it is imperative to catch readers' attention quickly, and to give them something at the end to engage their emotions.

There is a tremendous amount of written material in the world to choose from. Readers do not have time to twiddle their thumbs while you figure out what to say on a topic. They don't want to be distracted by poor grammar and punctuation, or have to strain to get the point being communicated. They want an immediate sense of what the writing means, and they want to feel it is important to them. Rewriting until every word and sentence is both easily understood and accomplishes an important task is the best way to hook and hold any reader's attention.

Although a research report submitted to a journal might certainly be rejected on the basis of being poorly written or uninteresting, you might think that trying to catch or "hook" the reader's interest in a *term paper* is superfluous. After all, teachers are the readers of term papers and they are required to read them. Right? Well, yes, teachers have to read term papers, but how much attention they give to them, and how much credit they give students for them, depends on whether they have been engaged by the writing or not. Term papers that are a struggle to read, that force a teacher to stop every few sentences and puzzle out the meaning, do not get good grades.

Your authors have read many term papers in their careers, both good and bad. There were commonalties in each. The good papers made some effort to capture our attention, to treat us like human beings instead of "professors." They showed evidence of care, evidence that the student had given some thought to what they were saying and how to say it. In short, they showed evidence of being rewritten, at least in the student's mind if not always on paper.

The bad papers? Well, there are many reasons why a paper might be bad, poor organization, poor punctuation and grammar, poor use of time by waiting until the last minute to start. The most common reason, though, is that the writer put down on paper the first things that came to mind concerning his or her topic, and then just left them that way.

To give an idea of what we mean by "good" and "bad" writing, we are going to give some examples and then try to explain why they are one or the other. All of these examples are shown exactly as they were taken from actual term papers handed in for grades at the university level. They are put inside quotation marks and used strictly for educational purposes. The names have been left out to protect the guilty. We are also going to go through a couple of rewriting exercises, again with examples taken from actual papers. All of this is part of the drafting process.

Good Examples of Opening Sentences
(Our comments follow, outside the quotation marks)

1. "The term mnemonics was invented by the ancient Greeks."
This paper opens with a factual statement, often an excellent way to start. Even if you stop reading at this point, you have learned something. The sentence also gives a clear statement as to what the paper is going to be about.

2. "Philosophers, poets, and scientists have long been intrigued by the relative influence of nature and nurture on human behavior."
This is an attempt at a "hook." And it works. The writer is trying to intrigue the reader into reading further. Philosophers, poets and scientists are quite different. Yet, this writer says that they are all fascinated by the same topic, "nature and nurture." What could be so interesting that three very different kinds of people want to understand it? This opening makes you want to know more.

3. "Many people go through the scenario of: 'Where are my keys, I forgot my glasses, I remember my first love.'"

This is a different kind of hook, an attempt to engage the reader by tying the paper to something—like memory lapses or the resurfacing of old memories—that almost everyone has directly experienced. Because most people would love to know why such things happen, this hook also works. Remember that not everyone is interested in psychology per se, but they are almost always interested in things having to do with their own lives, things that affect them.

Also remember, however, that the opening sentence of a paper is a kind of promise. In the sentence we are considering here, the writer is promising the reader that they will find out some interesting things about memory and forgetting. This promise must be fulfilled by the end of the paper or the reader will go away unsatisfied. That can mean a low grade if reader and teacher are the same person. If the reader is also a journal editor or any kind of publisher then the work will simply be rejected.

Bad Examples of Opening Sentences
(Again, our comments follow)

4. "Learning and memory play an important role in our lives."

This is a hook but it's too obvious to be a good one. Of course learning and memory play important roles in our lives. Everyone knows that! So why state it. It's much better to start with things most readers don't know.

This opening is also too general to really grab a reader's attention. It's like saying, "There sure was a lot of weather today." Does that mean rain, snow, or sunny skies? Instead, #3 under the good examples makes memory concrete and immediate by using specific situations like someone forgetting their keys or recalling a first love. Good writing is just that specific and concrete. It calls up visual images (or sounds, smells, and touches) that make the reader "see" what the writer has in mind.

Contrast, "It was a dreary day to ride the train" with "There were gray clouds and rain, and the few people on the train had faces as cold and heavy as grief." Which one connects you to the scene more strongly? Notice from the example just given that being specific can take up more room than being general, but the extra space is well spent if it lets you connect better with the reader.

5. "Memory as defined in the student's dictionary of psychology 'is the term given to the storage and subsequent retrieval of information.'"

There are a number of problems with this opening. First, it's incorrectly punctuated. There should be commas after "memory" and after "psychology." Second, dictionaries should generally not be used as references in term papers. A textbook definition would be better. Third, and most importantly, the writer is talking about information from one specific book but doesn't tell us what we need to know about that book.

The *Publication Manual of the American Psychological Association* (APA, 2001) requires that the use of other people's ideas and words be "cited" in the text. This means that the writer must state, usually in parentheses, the author(s) of the book and the date it was published. The title should be italicized and capitalized, and if a direct word-for-word quote is used it must be enclosed in quotation marks, must have the page number where it was found listed, and must match *exactly* the words from the source.

The words enclosed in quotation marks in the sample student paper are actually *different* from the words in the book they are taken from. Correctly rewritten and properly cited, the sentence would read: As defined in *A Student's Dictionary of Psychology* (Stratton and Hayes, 1988, p.

110), memory is "The general term given to the storage and subsequent retrieval of information."

6. "This paper entails the processing of information in memory and how works in humans. It involves notification of encoding, storage, and retrieval."

This example illustrates two common mistakes made by student writers. First, it shows that the student probably did not proofread. A quick scan would have shown that the word "it" is missing after the word "how." Second, the student also didn't bother to look up words of which he or she was unsure. Both "entails" and "notification" are used incorrectly, destroying any coherence these sentences might have had. Since it's another common error, this student *may* have tried to use the big words to sound more scholarly. It didn't work. Simpler words with clearer meanings would have been better.

7. "Even before man stood and walked on two legs, he had to progress to that state."

Excuse me! This sentence is incomprehensible. This doesn't mean the words are used incorrectly; it means they make no sense used together as they are here. Conceivably, this sentence could have something to do with evolution, but the paper it was taken from was a discussion of the effects of punishment on learning. The next two sentences were, "Man, through trial and error, gained knowledge and used this knowledge in his progression. This acquisition of knowledge through experience is deemed learning." This writer just covered millions of years in three sentences, and probably lost most readers along the way.

In addition, the writing here would actually be considered sexist by the APA. Not all humans are accurately described by words like "man" or "he." It used to be common to refer to the whole human race as "Man" or "Mankind." That's no longer true. "Humans, "humanity," or "humankind" would have been better word choices.

In regard to the examples we've just given, we should note that the students whose "bad" sentences we've taken were not at all bad writers. The paper that we just discussed, for example, improved steadily beyond the first paragraph and was able to earn a "C" grade. The problem is that most readers would have tossed the paper after the awful opening and would never have made it to the better stuff beyond. Even experienced writers write bad stuff sometimes. Most rough drafts are "bad stuff," which is the exact point of this chapter.

The difference between "A" and "C" papers is that "A" papers are rewritten, usually more than once. The best examples that we gave in this section were almost certainly rewritten. At least the students who wrote them took a little time to think about what they were writing. In fact, much "rewriting" does not take place on paper. It takes place in the head, before a word ever goes on a page. The writer just discards the thoughts that did not work and puts down the ones that did. What makes word processors so nice is that they allow you to do all that thinking on the screen. You can rewrite a sentence a dozen different ways and compare them before discarding the ones that don't work. Or, as many authors do, you can save all the extra versions in a separate file in case you later decide that some other wording was best.

Now that we've looked at some short examples to see what is right or wrong with them, the next step is to take a longer piece and try to make it better. The following two samples are opening paragraphs from actual papers. Each original paragraph appears first, and one possible rewrite is shown immediately after. Read both versions of the paragraph carefully, and then study the explanation that follows.

Sample 1: (Original;
Paper Entitled "Learned Helplessness")

"As the term learned helplessness has come to be understood, we use three criteria to recognize the phenomenon. First, learned helplessness is present when a person or animal displays inappropriate passivity: failing through lack of mental or behavioral action to meet the demands of a situation where effective coping is possible. Second, learned helplessness follows in the wake of uncontrollable events. As we emphasized earlier, bad events per se do not cause learned helplessness. Trauma may produce unfortunate reactions, including passivity, but trauma-induced helplessness is not of the "learned" variety. Third, learned helplessness is mediated by particular cognitions which are acquired during a person's exposure to new situations. As we noted before, the exact nature of these cognitions is unclear (Garber, 1980)."

Sample 1: (Rewrite)

(Problems with original = wordy, poor citations, confusing opening, awkward phrasing.)

If you've ever heard anyone say that they "just can't do math," because they failed at it in grade school, then you may well have met someone who suffers from learned helplessness. You may even be that someone. Learned helplessness occurs when people, or animals, give up trying to solve the kind of problems they have been unsuccessful at solving in the past (Seligman, 1975). There are three ways to recognize learned helplessness. First, the individual remains passive in situations where a solution to their problem is readily available. Second, such helplessness can usually be traced to bad events that happened in the individual's past (e.g., failing a first math class). Third, helplessness has a cognitive or thinking component to it. People *believe* that they cannot solve a certain type of problem or succeed in a certain type of situation (Seligman, 1975, 1991).

Sample 1: (Explanation)

The rewrite is a few words longer than the original but is also better in many ways. First, the opening grabs readers' attention by giving them a concrete example of learned helplessness, and by suggesting that helplessness might apply to someone they know, perhaps even themselves. Second, the third sentence of the rewrite provides a definition of learned helplessness for the reader to refer to. In the original, the reader was left to define helplessness on their own.

Third, the rewrite is in simpler, everyday language. Many students mistakenly believe that scientific writing must always be filled with multi-syllable words. This is absolutely not true. The first goal of writing is to communicate, not confuse. Fourth, the rewrite adds important references to Martin Seligman, who discovered learned helplessness and who has been a long-time theorist in the field. Fifth, and finally, the rewritten version is more clear and easier to read than the original. Simply breaking one paragraph into two made the piece easier to read, and this follows a modern trend toward shorter paragraphs.

There is one problem with the rewrite, though. It uses "you" where formal papers typically should not. Rewriting it without the "you" might give: "Some people who say they 'just can't do math,' because they failed at in high school, may well suffer from learned helplessness, and almost anyone can develop this problem under the right circumstances." There's nothing wrong with this opening, but the version that used "you" seems more powerful and maybe this is a time to disregard the "rules." Just know what the rules are before breaking them.

Sample 2: (Original;
Paper Entitled "Alzheimer's Disease")

"Learning and memory play an important role in our lives. Some point in life, an individual face a loss of memory. This deterioration of memory could be caused by a disease known as Alzheimer's disease. Alzheimer's disease is one of the most common diseases elderly people acquire. It is important for us to understand why an individual loses his/her memory. It is also important for us to understand that, if we lose our memory it effects our learning and memory. In this paper, I plan to discuss the following: What is Alzheimer's disease and what is its relation to learning and memory. The inheritance of Alzheimer's disease and the memory deficit of Alzheimer's disease according to dementia. The symptoms of the disease and how worse the disease can get."

Sample 2: (Rewrite)

(Problems with original = poor grammar and punctuation, missing words, no citations, awkward phrasing, did not proofread.)

Older people, those in their seventies and beyond, generally do not learn and remember information as easily as younger people. This is a generalization, of course, but many research studies strongly support this basic conclusion (see Botwinick, 1984 for a review). There are many possible explanations for the relatively poor performance of the elderly on learning and memory tasks. These range from an age-related increase in interference (knowing more total information makes it harder to store and retrieve one specific fact), to such pathological processes as Alzheimer's disease. The latter topic, Alzheimer's, is the subject of this paper. Some issues to be covered are 1) the causes of the disease, 2) the symptoms, 3) the possibility that Alzheimer's is partially inherited, and 4) the effects of the disease on learning and memory.

Sample 2: (Explanation)

In this example the rewrite is two sentences longer than the original, but the original really needed serious work. In fact, much of the original was probably unnecessary. If you're writing a term paper on Alzheimer's, why begin with a vague statement about people suffering from a loss of memory at some point during their lives. Given that the writer did start out that way, however, it needed to be made clear how aging, memory loss, and Alzheimer's disease could all be related. The rewrite makes this connection explicitly, and it shortens and clarifies the section that tells the reader what the paper is about.

You've now seen a couple of finished rewrites and have read some explanation of them, but this is no substitute for actual practice. There's no way, short of doing it, to figure out all the thought processes involved. Because of this, we'd like to use much of the remainder of this chapter to provide you with opportunities to do your own rewriting. By "providing you with opportunities," we mean, of course, giving you written assignments that have to be handed in for grades. We like to word things positively, however. For now, please complete the following assignments as indicated. The medicine is good for you, despite how it may taste.

Assignment 1

Using your own paper and informational sources like a dictionary and writing guide, rewrite the following sentences to remove the errors in grammar, punctuation and spelling, and to make the sentences themselves more clear. All but one of these samples were taken from actual works that were handed in for grades. Can you guess which one was created specifically for this book?

1. "When they are hungry or want to be held or need to be clean babies respond in there own way by crying or screeming."
2. "Lying is also used to conceal real truths, escape punishment, to save face, and to also shun responsibility."
3. "Suppression is the avoiding of thoughts that are stressful or negative in some sort of way by substituting them with other thoughts that are not so hurtful to the person."
4. "When we analyze dreams using Freudian methods we see that he considers there to be two different kinds of content found in a dream, manifest and latent."
5. "Some people can get by one just a few hours sleep while others require eight nine or more."

Assignment 2

Now, let's try rewriting something longer, like the following paragraph, again taken from an actual term paper. Start out by carefully reading the entire piece; then concentrate on correcting the errors in the original and trying to make the piece clearer. This is a difficult one, but struggle with it. See what you can do. And don't forget references.

1. "Dementia of Alzheimer's disease is a chemical syndrome referring to a loss of several mental functions

concerning intllectual, memory and personality of elderly people. The cognitive function begans to grow worse and the symptoms occur. The symptoms include forgetting, naming incompetence and spatial deteriorating. Although the symptoms may be different for each individual, most symptoms are caused by pathological changes. Once the symptoms occur, the person with Alzheimer's disease become extremely ill and the intellectual and basic functions get worse. With these results, the person dies."

Assignment 3

Rewrite the following paragraph, which is already much better than the previous example. Correct the errors, but also look at ways to make it even better, even such simple ways as breaking it into more paragraphs.

1. "Ivan Pavlov, a Russian physiologist, developed a procedure to study the way organisms learn about relationships between events in their environment. This procedure was called classical conditioning, which is a form of learning in which the behavior (conditioned response) comes to be elicited by a stimulus (conditioned stimulus) that has acquired its power through association with a biologically significant stimulus (unconditioned stimulus), also called Pavlovian or Respondent conditioning. In the classical conditioning paradigm, a biologically significant stimulus called unconditioned stimulus (US), elicits a reflex called unconditioned response (UR). A neutral stimulus that is then paired repeatedly with the conditioned stimulus (CS), is a stimulus capable of eliciting a similar response. This response elicited by a conditioned stimulus is called a conditioned response (CR) (Zimbardo, 1985)."

We are nearing the end of our discussion on rewriting but we have only just scratched the surface of the whole drafting process. We've tried to provide some general guidelines to follow—along with some practice—but guidelines won't help much unless they're put to work on your next writing project. If you want to be a *good* writer, instead of just an adequate one, then you simply must master the discipline needed to do multiple drafts. This is the best way to learn how to write, and the best way to make good grades while learning.

Before closing this chapter, there are three more topics that we want to touch on briefly. These are plagiarism, proofreading, and follow-up. A good rewriting job will help with the first two; the last depends on your own initiative.

Plagiarism

A seldom considered benefit of rewriting is that it almost ensures that you won't *plagiarize*. Plagiarism is stealing. It means taking someone else's words or ideas and using them without giving the original author credit. Plagiarism at the college level usually earns stiff penalties, from getting a zero on the paper itself, to failing the class, all the way up to expulsion from school. It is *not* a misdemeanor by academic standards.

Some of your authors know how bad it feels to be plagiarized because they've had their own works stolen by others. One found a paper that he'd published for sale at a "term paper mill," a website that sells papers to students so that they can put their own names on them and turn them in for class credit. Not only is that wrong, of course, but it's awfully lazy in addition. (And just imagine if a student had handed that paper in for credit to the professor who actually wrote it.)

Plagiarism demeans the academic and scientific process, but avoiding it is easy. *Quote* a specific passage word for word if you must. Just remember the quotation marks, and to give the page numbers where the passage appeared and the author's name who originated it. You can also "paraphrase," meaning to "summarize" or "reword" a passage. The rewording should be fairly substantial, however, and even in paraphrasing you still need to indicate the name of the person whose ideas you are borrowing from.

You can't rewrite quotes, but rewriting what you paraphrase will make sure that it differs substantially from the original source. And if you like someone else's ideas and want to mention them in your paper, just give credit where credit is due. Above all, don't be so lazy that you're willing to pay for a stolen paper. That's not going to help you learn how to write for yourself, and it could cost much more than the price of the report. Some people lose careers because of plagiarism.

Proofreading

Proofreading is the last thing to do before handing in a term paper or sending off a research report. It's really the final stage of the drafting process, but it takes place *after* you think the paper is finished. We suggest actually printing a copy of what you believe to be the finished paper because some mistakes are easier to catch in hard copy. Once you've printed the project, and do so on scrap paper so you won't mind marking changes, read through the entire thing again. Go line by line and check for errors. At this point, the hard work is finished. The paper is as clear and coherent as you can get it. But, even though there are no substantial changes left to make, there probably are some minor errors still present, most likely in spelling, punctuation, or phrasing. Proofreading helps catch these minor lapses.

The key to good proofreading is to *not* read the paper for coherence and meaningfulness. Don't allow yourself to get caught up in the "story line" of the paper. That work has already been done during the drafting process. What you want now is to see if the words and phrasings are themselves correct. If you read only to see if the paper makes overall sense, then your mind will automatically correct misspellings, supply missing words, and translate awkward phrases. Your mind knows what you meant to say; you have to check to make sure that you really did say it.

Because it's often difficult to separate the structure of the words from their meaning within the paper, good proofreaders have come up with some strategies to help. One very effective strategy is to start with the last sentence and read backwards toward the first. This prevents you from getting caught up in the "story line" and forces you to pay attention to the words and phrases in isolation from the rest of the paper. A second strategy, also excellent, is to put the paper away for a few days and let it lose its immediacy. You may then be able to look at it line by line without being overwhelmed by the meaning and by your own memory of what you *intended* to say. Finally, you can always ask a trustworthy friend to proofread for you.

What do you do when you've already proofread and printed the final copy of a term paper and then find a minor error on your way to a professor's office to turn it in? You don't have to go back and reprint a new copy. Instead, carefully and neatly pencil in the correction(s). If a word is misspelled, make one line through it with a pencil and then print the correct spelling immediately above it. Even phrases can be corrected this way, as long as the entire paragraph doesn't have to be marked up. For a research report or scholarly paper submitted to a journal, however, reprint rather than make handwritten corrections. Keep submissions as professional looking as possible.

Follow-Up

Once the proofreading is done and a term paper is in an instructor's hands, you might think that all the work is finished. Not quite. No matter how hard you tried, the paper still won't be perfect. Proofreading may have caught most of the misspellings and grammatical gaffes, but there will probably be errors in organization and clarity, places where you didn't completely understand the material, or places where some important piece of information got left out simply because you didn't know about it. This is where follow-up comes into play.

Most teachers either hand back papers with comments written on them, or are willing to sit down with students and discuss the good and bad points of a paper. You need that feedback to get better as a writer. When you get a paper back, study it. Forget the grade; that's already in the past. Read the comments written by the teacher and go ask for an explanation of anything that isn't clear. Even if a teacher does not hand back papers, go and ask for an explanation of your mistakes. Ask nicely and the teacher will probably be thrilled to know that you care about improving your work.

Journals, of course, will either reject a submission out right, or they will provide comments from other researchers (peer reviewers) who have examined the work and then ask for a resubmission. They won't correct your grammar—if the grammar is too bad you'll get an automatic rejection—but they will probably make suggestions about the content, length, focus, references, and analyses in the paper. These, too, can be very helpful sources of feedback to help improve your writing.

Conclusions

We are now at the end of this chapter, and almost at the end of this *Guidebook*. The last chapter is mainly a checklist to compare your papers against before handing them in. There are also the supplementals, the Appendix, Bibliography, and Glossary, and you should certainly take a look at them, but most of the meat of the book is now finished. Having read this book does not make you a great writer. There are no magic formulas to accomplish that feat. We do hope that all of you have found something in this text to use, and we hope that at least some of you have found out how rewarding it is to write well.

CHAPTER TEN

CONCLUSIONS (A FINAL DRAFT CHECKLIST)

"The time to begin writing an article is when you have finished it to your satisfaction. By that time you begin to clearly and logically perceive what it is you really want to say."
—Mark Twain

Before turning in a paper or mailing one off to a journal, there are a number of things to check one last time, either on the computer screen or by hand on a printed copy. If errors are present and you don't find them, then the journal editor or your teacher certainly will. And he or she may hold them against you when it comes time to accept the work or to assign a grade.

This last chapter consists primarily of a list of those things that need to be checked. Make copies of this list, which appears on the next few pages, and try to compare each of your papers against it. The results should be better writing and more professional papers. It sure won't hurt your grade either.

Checklist

Put a check beside each step as it's completed.

__1. Proofread for errors, which includes word by word checking of grammar and spelling. As we said in Chapter 9, it would be great if, after finishing a paper, you could let it sit for a day or two before giving it the final proofreading. This makes it much easier to catch mistakes.

__2. Check the paper's format, whether it's APA style or something else. Get a manual—most standard format manuals can be found in most college libraries, or can be purchased at the university bookstore—and go through the manuscript carefully to see if there are errors. In APA style, pay special attention to:

__a. Title Page: (title, your name, university name, running head, page header and page number 1).

__b. Page header: (the actual header appears on *every* page).

__c. Page numbers: (numbers on *every* page, 5 spaces after the page header).

__d. Reference format, both in text and in the reference list: (see also Chapter 2, and the *Publication Manual of the American Psychological Association*.)

__3. Double-check the submission requirements. Different journals and professors require different things (e.g., folders, staples, rough drafts, etc.), so make sure that what you submit is *exactly* what is being asked for. A sure way to earn a rejection or a low grade is to give your editors or professors something they didn't want and which makes their job more difficult.

__4. Make sure all references appear in at least two places in the paper, in the reference list and in the body of the paper. The *only* exceptions are for personal communications and for secondary sources (see Chapter 2 and the APA's *Publication Manual*).

__5. Check to see that encyclopedias or dictionaries (except for specialty dictionaries like medical dictionaries) have not been used as references. There should also be few citations to popular magazines and books, or to newspapers. Remember our cautions in Chapter 2 about the internet.

__6. If you've used quotations, which should only be used sparingly, then make sure the proper quotation marks ("") have been added, or that the appropriate text is set off from the rest. Someone else's exact words must be clearly marked as such or it is considered plagiarism (see Chapter 9). Also make sure that any quote used is word for word. Don't change another writer's language, even to correct an error.

If you feel that an error in the original source might cause confusion for the reader, call attention to the error without correcting it by writing the word "*sic*" immediately after the error in the quotation. The *sic* should be italicized and placed in brackets. Example: "Measurements were taken in reel [*sic*] time."

__7. Although not one of the most important tasks, do check to see that proper spacing has been used after periods, commas, and other forms of punctuation. One of the more common errors is failing to space between the ends of sentences and the start of citations in text (e.g., "...rats in mazes"(Smith, 1992)). There should be a space after the last quotation mark.

__8. After the paper is printed, read it out loud one last time. This will help in proofreading and will also ensure that you haven't lost a paragraph somewhere, or perhaps transposed a couple of pages. It happens all the time.

__9. Make a personal hard copy of the finished paper and then put it where it can be found again. You'll want it someday, either because you are doing another paper on the same topic and need the references, or because your teacher's dog ate the copy that you gave to him or her.

__10. If possible, hand term papers personally to a teacher. If not, make very sure to put it in the place where it is supposed to go. Students lose papers every year by sticking them in the wrong box or sliding them under the door to the wrong office. If you are submitting to a journal, make sure to address a cover letter for the manuscript directly to the journal's editor. Names of editors can usually be found in the front few pages of a journal or magazine where things like copyright notices and publication dates are given.

__11. *Relax*, but only until you get the paper back with comments on it. Then follow-up to see what you did right and wrong (see Chapter 9). And remember that your professor or a journal editor may not have caught or noted everything wrong with the manuscript. Correct your *own* errors.

APPENDIX A

TIME MANAGEMENT SCHEDULE

See Chapter 1 and Chapter 6 for discussion.

DATE: _____

Name: _____

	TIME	M	T	W	TH	F	S	SU
AM	8:00							
	9:00							
	10:00							
	11:00							
PM	12:00							

1:00							
2:00							
3:00							
4:00							
5:00							
6:00							
7:00							
8:00							
9:00							
10:00							

	11:00							
AM	12:00							
	1:00							
	2:00							
	3:00							
	4:00							
	5:00							
	6:00							

	7:00							

BIBLIOGRAPHY

This Bibliography is divided into two sections. Section 1 contains books that can be used as "tools" to help you write better. These are books you'll use every day and which will need to be kept handy on your desk. Some of them you may already have (or at least their equivalents). Section 2 contains books that deal with the issues of words, language, and writing in a more general way. Many of these are fun to read as well as being helpful with the subtleties of our English tongue. Some of these books may also exist in newer editions than are listed here.

(Note: if you need some examples of APA's reference style, you can follow the entries in this Bibliography and in the Reference list itself for this book.)

Section 1: Tool Books.

1. The writer's best tool is a general purpose dictionary. Two good ones are:

Ehrlich, E., Flexner, S. B., Carruth, G., & Hawkins, J. M. (eds.). (1982). *Oxford American dictionary* (reissue ed.). New York: Avon.
Guralnik, D. B. (Ed. in Chief). (1986). *Webster's new world dictionary of the American language* (2nd ed.). New York: Prentice Hall Press.

2. You may also want a specialized dictionary in your field, such as:

Hayes, N., & Stratton, P. (2003). *A student's dictionary of psychology* (4th ed.). London: Hodder Arnold.

3. Another good tool is a thesaurus in dictionary form, such as:

Laird, C. (Ed.). (2003). *Webster's new world thesaurus* (Reissue ed.). New York: Pocket.
Morehead, P. D. (Ed.). (2001). *New American Roget's college thesaurus in dictionary form*. New York: Signet.

4. You will certainly want a guide to help with punctuation and grammar. There are many such books, but a good one is:

Shertzer, M. (1996). *The elements of grammar* (Subsequent ed.). New York: Longman.

5. For those problem words and phrases, try the following:

Shaw, H. (1987). *Dictionary of problem words and expressions* (Rev. ed.). New York: McGraw-Hill.
Strunk, W., Jr., & White, E. B. (1979). *The elements of style* (3rd ed.). New York: Macmillan Publishing Co., Inc. (Note: There is a 4th edition of this but the 3rd is more commonly cited.)

Section 2: General books dealing with writing related issues.

Claiborne, R. (1983). *Our marvelous native tongue*. New York: Times Books.

Dunn, D. S. (2007). *Short guide to writing about psychology* (2nd ed.). New York: Longman.

Day, R. A., & Gastel, B. (2006). *How to write and publish a scientific paper* (6th ed.). Westport, CT: Greenwood Publishing Group.

Fowler, H. W. (1965). *A dictionary of modern English usage* (2nd ed.). New York: Oxford University Press.

Fulwiler, T. (2002). *College writing: A personal approach to academic writing* (3rd ed.). Portsmouth, NH: Boynton/Cook Publishers.

Gordon, K. E. (1983). *The well-tempered sentence*. New York: Ticknor & Fields.

Gordon, K. E. (1984). *The transitive vampire*. New York: Times Books.

Johnson, E. D. (1982). *The handbook of good English*. New York: Facts on File Publications.

Katz, M. J. (1985). *Elements of the scientific paper*. New Haven: Yale University Press.

Landrum, R. E. (2008). *Undergraduate writing in psychology: Learning to tell the scientific story*. Washington, DC: American Psychological Association.

Lester, J. D., & Lester, J. D., Jr. (2004). *Writing research papers: A complete guide* (11th ed.). New York: Longman.

Luey, B. (2002). *Handbook for academic authors* (4th ed.). Cambridge, MA: Cambridge University Press.

McCrum, R., Cran, W., & MacNeil, R. (1986). *The story of English*. New York: Elisabeth Sifton Books—Viking.

Meyer, M. (1985). *The little brown guide to writing research papers*. Boston: Little Brown.

Mitchell, M. L., Jolley, J. M., & O'Shea, R. P. (2009). *Writing for psychology*. Belmont, CA: Wadsworth Publishing Company.

Newman, E. (1974). *Strictly speaking*. New York: Warner Books.

Newman, E. (1975). *A civil tongue*. New York: The Bobbs-Merril Company, Inc.

Plotnik, A. (1986). *The elements of editing* (Reissue ed.). New York: Macmillan Publishing Co.

Rosnow, R. L., & Rosnow. M. (2005). *Writing papers in psychology* (7th ed.). Belmont, CA: Wadsworth Publishing Company.

Safire, W. (1990). *Fumblerules*. New York: Bantam Doubleday Dell Publishing Group, Inc.

Soukhanov, A. H. (Executive Ed.). (1986). *Word mysteries & histories*. Boston, MA: Houghton Mifflin Company.

Train, J. (1980). *Remarkable words with astonishing origins*. New York: Clarkson N. Potter, Inc.

Zinsser, W. (2006). *On writing well* (30th anv. ed.). New York: HarperCollins Publishers.

Section 3: A few helpful web sites.

http://www.apastyle.org/stylehelper/ --APA style helper. Software for purchase.

http://www.dictionary.com --Lots of good writing help.

http://www.psy.pdx.edu/PsiCafe/ --The Psyc Café, a great student resource.

http://www.xula.edu/library/ --The Xavier Library

GLOSSARY

Abstract: a brief paragraph (up to 250 words) summarizing the major points of a study or experiment. It generally includes information on independent and dependent variables, numbers and types of subjects used, and the most important results (see the *Publication Manual of the American Psychological Association*).

Abstract Journal: a collection of abstracts from a specific field of research (i.e., psychology, biology, etc.). They usually come out once a month and report on recent research in their area of coverage. *Psychological Abstracts*, which is an example, contains a complete listing (author, title, etc.) of articles published in American Psychological journals each month, and provides an abstract of the article as well. Increasingly, these are available through online databases. See also *Dissertation Abstracts International*.

APA Style: a standard style protocol used by a number of social sciences; this style dictates appropriate language use in terms of grammar, manuscript construction, and overall written expression.

Bibliography: a list of articles or books that are concerned with a specific topic. These are often found at the end of science books under the title of "A Guide to Further Reading." A bibliography is not the same as a references list. The term "references" refers to all, *and only*, those books and articles that were used in actually writing a paper. A bibliography, on the other hand, can contain books that were not cited, but which readers of a paper might also find of interest. APA style requires references, not a bibliography.

Citation: occurs any time a journal article or book (or even a newspaper article) is referred to in print, whether it be in a term paper or in another article or book. These are also referred to as "citations in text," and in APA style they usually take the form of: 1) "According to Ames and Sallis (1999)..." or 2) "As indicated by some writers (Proctor, Bonner, & Lanoue, 1997)...." Any information taken from another source must be cited, and all such citations must appear both in the References section of the paper and in the body of the paper. (See Personal Communications & Secondary Sources for the *only* exceptions to this rule.)

Database: a collection of periodical abstracts or articles that is stored on a computer. This means that you can let the computer help with the hard work of finding sources. To conduct a search, enter a few key words and let the computer sift through the thousands of entries in the database to find any abstracts or articles that use those words. For example, enter "cocaine" and "rat," and the computer will find all the database entries that look at the effects of cocaine in rats. Then refine the search with more keywords. Some database searches involve a fee, though the cost may be worth it considering the savings in time and effort. Many database searches are free to students and faculty members at universities. PsycINFO is an example of a database.

Discussion: an evaluation and interpretation of the results from a study or experiment. This is the section of a research paper that tells the reader what was found in the study, how those findings match up with what was expected (the hypothesis), and why the findings are of interest and importance (see the *Publication Manual*).

Dissertation Abstracts International: a comprehensive collection of dissertation abstracts from many disciplines. A dissertation is the original research or scholarly project that Ph.D. candidates must complete before being awarded the doctorate degree. These abstracts can be useful as references for a term paper or research report, but remember that these are not complete manuscripts. Some online databases, such as ProQuest, also provide access to dissertation abstracts.

Header: see Manuscript Page Header

Interlibrary Loan: a process by which a library that lacks a certain book or journal can borrow the needed material from another library that has it. For example, if you need a special book that your library doesn't own, then you can still borrow the book through interlibrary loan. Both university and public libraries have facilities for interlibrary loan.

Introduction: the opening part of a paper or report. In a research report, the Introduction contains a review of the relevant literature and a description of the overall design and purpose of the experiment. It makes a specific statement about the hypothesis that is being tested. This is not generally true of a term paper, however. A term paper consists mainly of a review of the literature, with some attempt at analysis and synthesis. For example, a term paper on schizophrenia would examine and discuss as many books and journal articles on the subject as possible, and would then try to draw some conclusions from the facts that were presented. A term paper *might* be a research report, but this would be unusual.

Journal: the magazine of the scientific world. Journals can appear from two to four times a year up to once a month. They generally focus on a single topic (e.g., *Brain Research* or *Pharmacology, Biochemistry and Behavior*). Unlike magazines, however, most journals receive little financial support from subscriptions. They are purely scholarly, with the focus being on the sharing of information in a specialized field. "Peer-reviewed" journals are considered the standard in science. Articles published in these journals are first reviewed by prominent researchers (peers) in the field, and then revised based upon input from those peers.

Journal Article: A journal article usually reports the specifics of an empirical study, and in this case is also called a "research report." Journal articles may also review a large number of studies in one area, however, in which case they are called "review articles," or they may address a substantial theoretical issue in the field, as in "theoretical articles." Term papers are usually most similar to review articles.

Manuscript Page Header: a truncated title (consisting of the first two or three words of the title) with page numbers, which allows a reader to reassemble a manuscript in the event that its pages become separated.

Method: a section of a research paper that describes in detail how a study or experiment was carried out. It contains subsections on participants/subjects, apparatus, procedure, and it may have sections on design or analysis. The purpose of the Method section is to let other scientists see exactly what you did in a study, and to replicate that work if they wish. Term papers do not have a Method section unless they are, in fact, an actual experiment (see the *Publication Manual*).

Monograph: a book that focuses on a specific topic, such as Alzheimer's disease or anorexia nervosa. Monographs are usually edited books containing chapters written by different authors, but it is becoming more common to refer to any scientific book as a monograph.

Periodical: written material released "periodically," as in once a month, or four times a year. In library usage, the term generally refers to journals, magazines, and newspapers. There will be a separate area in the library where the periodicals are kept.

Plagiarism: using someone else's words or ideas without giving them proper credit. This is a *serious* offense.

Personal Communications: anything that is "told" to you but which does not appear in a public and written form is considered a personal communication. This would include information from private letters and emails, phone conversations, and from personal interactions, such as when a professor tells you some information in a lecture or in his or her office. Personal communications appear only in the text of a paper and not in the reference list (see Chapter 2).

PsycINFO: an online database that directs the user to the journal, volume, and edition that holds an article on a particular topic. It contains abstracts for all articles and full text links to some.

References: see "Bibliography" above, and the *Publication Manual*.

Running Head: see "Title Page" in this glossary, and the *Publication Manual*.

Results: a straightforward report of the findings from an experiment or study. It usually contains a verbal description of the experimental results (e.g., was the original hypothesis supported or not), and it bolsters the verbal description with a statistical analysis (e.g., an ANOVA). Data from the results, such as means and standard deviations, are often reported in tables, graphs, and figures (see the *Publication Manual*).

Secondary Sources: when you read about an individual's original ideas or research in a source other than the original it is called a secondary source. Reading *about* Sigmund Freud's theory of the superego in a book by "Lana Rose" is an example. Freud would be the primary source, Rose the secondary. In the body of the paper both the primary and secondary sources are indicated, but in the reference list only the secondary source should appear. That's the one you actually read. Every effort should be made to use primary sources whenever possible (see Chapter 2.)

Title Page: page number 1 of a journal article or term paper. Centered on this page will be the title of the article, followed by the author's name on the next line, and by the author's location (usually a university) on the line below that. It is possible to have several authors, but include no more than two locations. Somewhere above the title and flush left there should appear the words "Running head:," followed by a short version of the title typed in all capital letters. This running head (i.e., the short title) is often the same as the "Manuscript Page Header," and, if so, should also appear at the top right next to the page number on every page of the paper except for those pages where figures appear, if figures are used. As a "Header," however, only the first letters of the words should be capitalized (see the *Publication Manual*).

REFERENCES

American Psychiatric Association. (2000). *Diagnostic and statistical manual of mental disorders* (4th ed., Text Revision). Washington, DC: Author

American Psychological Association. (2001). *Publication manual of the American Psychological Association* (5th ed.). Washington, DC: Author.

Boller, P. F. (1996). *Not so!: Popular myths about America from Columbus to Clinton.* New York: Oxford University Press, USA.

Botwinick, J. (1984). *Aging and behavior* (3rd ed.). New York: Springer Publishing Company, Inc.

Dunn, D. S. (2001, February). *Writing in research methods, methods for research writing.* Invited presentation at the 13th Annual Southeastern Conference on the Teaching of Psychology, Atlanta, GA.

Fryxell, D. A. (2001). Those elusive first words. *Writer's Digest, 81*(9), 24-25, 62.

Gay, P. (1988). *Freud: A life for our time.* New York: W. W. Norton & Company.

Hemingway, E. (1952). *The old man and the sea.* New York: Charles Scribner's Sons.

King, Stephen. (2000). *On writing.* New York: Pocket Books.

Lynn, K. S. (1987). *Hemingway.* New York: Simon and Schuster.

Meyer, R. G., & Salmon, P. (1988). *Abnormal psychology* (2nd ed.). Boston: Allyn and Bacon, Inc.

Pasachoff, J. M. (1987). *Astronomy: From the Earth to the Universe* (3rd ed.). New York: Saunders College Publishing.

Schultz, D. P., & Schultz, S. E. (1987). *A history of modern psychology* (4th ed.). New York: Harcourt Brace Jovanovich, Publishers.

Seligman, M. E. P. (1975). *Helplessness: On depression, development and death*. San Francisco: Freeman.

Seligman, M. E. P. (1991). *Learned optimism*. New York: Knopf.

Shaw, H. (1987). *Dictionary of problem words and expressions* (Rev. ed.). New York: McGraw-Hill.

Stratton. P., & Hayes, N. (1988). *A student's dictionary of psychology*. New York: Edward Arnold

Strunk, W., Jr., & White, E. B. (1979). *The elements of style* (3rd ed.). New York: Macmillan Publishing Co., Inc.

Underwood, T., & Miller, C. (Eds.). (1988). *Bare bones: Conversations on terror with Stephen King*. New York: McGraw-Hill.

Zinsser, W. K. (1990). *On Writing Well* (4th ed.). New York: HarperCollins Publishers.

INDEX

ABOUT THE AUTHORS

CHARLES ALLEN GRAMLICH grew up on a farm in Arkansas but moved to the New Orleans area in 1986 to teach psychology at Xavier University of Louisiana. He has an MS and PhD in Experimental Psychology from the University of Arkansas. Charles is an editor for *The Dark Man: The Journal of Robert E. Howard Studies*, and produces a regular column on writing for an online newsletter called *The Illuminata*. He's the author of *Write With Fire*, a book on the craft of writing, and has had four novels and numerous short stories published, mostly in the genres of horror, science fiction, and fantasy. He also writes non-fiction and poetry. Charles lives with his wife, Lana, in Abita Springs, Louisiana, and has a son named Joshua. His blog is at: http://charlesgramlich.blogspot.com/

ELLIOT D. HAMMER is an Associate Professor of Psychology and the John LaFarge Professor in Social Justice at Xavier University of Louisiana. He is currently serving as chairperson of the Psychology Department. Elliott earned his BA in Psychology at the University of Kansas and his MS and PhD in Experimental Social Psychology at Tulane University. He works extensively with students in research endeavors, exploring issues of stereotyping and person perception. Elliott reserves some time for his wife Elizabeth, their pets, traveling, and the music, food, and culture of New Orleans.

Y. DU BOIS IRVIN earned a PhD in Social Psychology from the University of Colorado at Boulder in 1979, then did a clinical internship in Houston, Texas. She taught in the Psychology Department at Xavier University of Louisiana for eighteen years. During that time she helped develop Xavier's Psychology-Premedical program, and also established Xavier's current chapter of Psi Chi, the national honors society in psychology. Du Bois is the granddaughter of W. E. B. Du Bois.

CPSIA information can be obtained
at www.ICGtesting.com
Printed in the USA
LVOW11s2341171116
513510LV00001B/8/P